SMALL

For Andrea
A kindred spirit!

Best,
[signature]

SMALL

the little we need
for happiness

jane anne staw

shanti arts publishing

brunswick, maine

Small: The Little We Need for Happiness

Published by Shanti Arts Publishing
Cover and interior design by Shanti Arts Designs

Shanti Arts LLC
Brunswick, Maine
www.shantiarts.com

Printed in the United States of America

First Edition

Lyrics of "One Day at a Time" written by
Marijohn Wilkin and Kris Kristofferson and
used with permission of Buckhorn Music

Cover image by Jane Ann Staw
Interior drawings of trees, branch,
and leaf by Nathan Maffin

"My Juliette Binoche" was previously published
in *SNReview*, Winter/Spring, 2011

ISBN: 978-1-947067-14-1 (softcover)
ISBN: 978-1-947067-26-4 (digital)

LCCN: 2017962949

For Amelie and Izel Poppy,
who ever since they were tiny,
have brought me incomparable joy

*This book owes so very much to Clara Snead,
an incomparable friend, reader and writer;
and to Victoria Pryor, my agent and friend,
who has always believed in my writing.*

Contents

PREFACE

SEVERAL YEARS AGO, AN IDEA FOUND ME AS I WAS
walking my dog Daphne around the block: Explore what happens
when you redirect your gaze to small. Though I wasn't sure
exactly what this shift would entail, I understood the concept
immediately. As l went about my quite ordinary days, instead of
wrestling with the problems I perceived in my own life and in the
life of my country — which I tended to inflate — I would make an
effort to bring my attention back to the smaller, positive moments
that usually drifted quickly through my consciousness, entering
and exiting within seconds.

Walking Daphne was a twice-daily activity, once in the morning
and once in the afternoon, always the same block, the same
direction. The walk was so ingrained, so familiar, so automatic
that I had stopped paying any real attention. While I did notice
obvious changes in the neighborhood — a house being painted, a
new garden installation, a shiny new car — for most of my route I
was only half conscious of my surroundings, walking in a state of
near-suspended observation.

Then one afternoon, I noticed a single, dried leaf on the
sidewalk, twisted in on itself, and suddenly I felt awareness course

through me, as if every cell had been awakened by the sight of that tiny, desiccated leaf. My whole body hummed with pleasure. At first there were no words, simply the physical sensation, a shiver of delight. Then, a few seconds after the shiver, I thought: *How beautiful that leaf is, how poignant; it looks balletic, as if its position has been choreographed.* It was then that the idea of thinking small first took hold of me.

I've never been known among my friends for thinking small. Until that very moment, my mind usually moved in the opposite direction. The minute the smallest event went awry or the tiniest worry pricked me, I leapt to huge and disastrous conclusions. In college, I was an all-or-nothing studier, believing that my options were either As or Fs, nothing in between. Given that choice, I found it necessary to sit nearly constantly at my desk, reading and rereading assigned texts, revising and re-revising term papers, going over and over the identical material for midterms and final exams. When I was pregnant, I couldn't imagine giving birth to a healthy baby. I thought about all that could go wrong from inception to birth. On a good day, my baby would be missing a finger or toe. On a bad day, my child would suffer from spina bifida or autism.

My life has not been a series of disasters. I did well in high school, learned to speak fluent French while living with a French family one summer in Paris, and I got into the college of my choice. Still, I thought of my life as a series of disasters averted. Constantly anticipating the worst, I ducked as I moved forward into the future, certain that unless I remained perpetually vigilant and performed everything as perfectly as possible, I would deserve to fail, to lose my way, to fall off the edge of the earth.

By the time the idea of thinking small came to me, I had made some progress against my tendency to catastrophize. Life had taught me a few lessons. The most important was patience. Things might go wrong, but that didn't mean they would stay wrong forever. If I didn't land the teaching position of my choice, for example, I wasn't doomed professionally; it might just turn out that my life would change, and perhaps I would become a writer because of someone I met at the school where I was hired. If as a child, my son, Jonah, tried my patience with his incessant negotiating, he might be developing the very skill that would serve him later as an entrepreneur. If only a few of my poems were accepted for publication, it didn't mean I would never get published; one day I might try my pen at essays, and these would find their way to the printed page.

These developments all took time, of course. And it wasn't until I reached a certain age that I could look back and see that some events or circumstances that had dismayed me at one point were remedied or transformed positively at another. But I had to learn to wait, to hold this truth close to my heart and soul . . . and be patient.

I began to think of life as a novel with distinct chapters, each having a beginning, middle, and end, but whose overall conclusion was only virtual. It hovered out there, somewhere in the future, and what it held might someday affect the way I felt about events and moments in my past. This was not only true of my life, but the lives of others as well. For years, my ex-husband's uncle mourned the loss of his relationship with his brother and his brother's family after the two had a falling out and his brother refused ever to speak to him again. Then his brother died, and the brother's daughter contacted the uncle when her son was born. "Joshua will never know his grandfather, but I want him to know his grandfather's brother."

A client of mine was a graduate student when she gave a daughter up for adoption at birth. Once she was married and had a family, my client felt wrenched by her earlier decision. How could she have given away a child? Then, when that daughter was in her thirties, she contacted her birth mother, and it turned out they were both writers. Once reunited, the two shared a central part of their lives, sending each other chapters from their novels and creating joint writing retreats several times a year.

The patience I gained to give life a chance to create its own wondrous stories was an important phase in my evolution. Now I am completing another transformation, wrought by that unexpected and unsolicited idea to think small. Since the initial idea found me, I have come to appreciate the significance of an idea that began as something small, then became a central practice in my life.

At first I set about thinking small by reminding myself to notice pockets of beauty in the natural world as I went about my day: the loft of a cloud formation, the grace of a vining rose, the sweep of wild grass in the breeze. But I quickly realized that I was limiting myself to my vision and forgetting about the rest of me. And while my pleasure at these small sights was authentic, it was actually unidimensional.

So I began paying attention to my whole being's response — mind, heart, body, and spirit — to moments I might otherwise have thought inconsequential, or have acknowledged with only a passing thought: *how sweet, how clever, how lovely.* Instead of moving quickly to the next moment, the next person, the next task, instead of moving past one sweet moment, I allowed my attention to remain with these moments. And when I did, I discovered that they penetrated, settling fathoms within me, then swelling to their full and rightful size, allowing me to experience an expansive joy, a profound happiness. A server's casual "That was so nice of you" after I helped a man in a wheelchair settle down with his coffee and muffin, led me deep into the Amazon of my soul as I explored whether my behavior had been altruistic or not. The smile of a stranger on a day I was feeling depressed and alienated revealed both how lonely I am at times and how easily I am able to feel a strong connection with others.

I have been thinking small for several years now, and the practice has taught me valuable lessons. First, I understand that there is so much more to celebrate each day than I ever believed possible: the trill of a junco, a casual comment by a friend, a ceramic vase sitting on my coffee table. When my attention lingered, the junco's song transported me to the Iowa countryside, the friend's casual comment settled in a place deep within me, and the vase bathed me in awe at the artist's ability to create an object of such beauty.

Second, paying attention to small has taught me that, if given permission, what I might initially perceive as minuscule might grow into an idea of importance to me or to someone I love. A mother's parting comment about her disabled child held in my mind for several minutes led me from thinking about the heroism of the mother to understanding the importance of appreciating even our smallest gifts. Mulling over an offhand story about holding dinner parties on a bed in a minuscule dorm room transported my mind from focusing on the inventiveness of the host to realizing just how often we overlook the possibilities that float around us. Stopping for several moments to watch a junco alight on a branch returned me not only to Proust but to Iowa and a chance to remember things in my past.

People often speak of the benefits of living in the moment, of being more present in the world. For each of us, being present offers a unique and individual experience. After all, how can you know who you really are if you are not fully aware of just how you respond to what is right before you? During the past few years of thinking small, I have been able to know and appreciate myself more completely than ever before. I have learned so much about what makes me the most keenly happy, the most thoughtful and reflective. And at the same time, thinking small has led me to appreciate and celebrate the gifts other people and the world have to offer.

The essays that follow are meditations and exercises in thinking small. The experiences they evoke sprang up in all facets of my life: my relationships, teaching, cooking, gardening, family, friends, and even my writing. And although the essays deal mainly with recent moments of small, they are not chronological. Each essay captures my shift from a moment of pleasure and appreciation to enduring joy; or from anger, depression, overwhelm, or loneliness to affection, calm, and connection. My hope is that while each essay transforms a simple experience, either positive or negative, into a source of profound contentment and wellbeing, this entire collection of essays progresses toward helping the reader find her place in what I have discovered to be a most welcoming universe. ▪

PART ONE:

SEEING SMALL

ONE DAY AT A TIME

Now that I've entered its universe, I am beginning to feel like a magnet for small. Some days ago, one of my clients explained that in an attempt to calm her anxiety over the new seminar she is teaching, she invoked a Russian proverb: "Little drops of water wear down a big stone." And a therapist friend told me about a client who recently inherited $15,000 from her father. This client has been on welfare most of her adult life, and this is the first time she has any discretionary money. "The problem is," my friend said, "she's been blinded by the sum."

No sooner had she been told about her inheritance, than my friend's client went on a shopping spree and spent over $1,000 on clothes for a party she had been invited to, but subsequently decided not to attend. "And now," my friend sighed, "she wants another $1,000 to begin her Christmas shopping."

My friend was concerned for her client, worried that within several months, the woman would have spent her entire inheritance and find herself right back where she had begun: completely dependent on the state, with not even one dollar of her own money. "If I could only figure out how to help her think small," my friend sighed.

The next day, on my way home from a wedding shower in San Francisco, I was listening to an NPR program on the history of their StoryCorps project, when the announcer introduced a tape made in 1993 by LeAlan Jones, at the time an eleven-year-old boy, and his grandmother, June Marie Jones. Toward the end of the tape, LeAlan requests that his grandmother sing her favorite hymn. She protests that her voice is "all messed up," but LeAlan insists, "Do it," and begins counting, "One . . . two . . . three." The grandmother responds and delivers the entire hymn "One Day at a Time," her voice dipping and cracking through the verses and the refrain, and finally fading out at the end.

> *Do you remember when you walked among men*
> *Well Jesus you know*
> *If you're lookin' below, it's worse now than then*
> *Pushin' and shovin' and crowdin' my mind*
> *So for my sake, teach me to take*
> *One day at a time*[1]

As soon as his grandmother's voice trails off, LeAlan comments, "She was hoarse, but she still can blow." And then there is silence.

Thinking this was the end of the interlude, I began reflecting on how the hymn LeAlan's grandmother sang converged in such a timely way with my own life, reminding me not to crowd my mind with too many desires, but to think small, to take one day at a time. But then, LeAlan's voice, now years later, deeper and more resonant, began speaking again — directly to me it seemed — about the original tape's importance for him. He and his family listen to it all the time, he said, and it is as if his grandmother is not only with them again, but singing to them. "If I only had this — and nothing else — it would be enough," he concluded.

To affirm that something, any one thing, might hold for

---

1. Marijohn Wilkin and Kris Kristofferson, Buckhorn Music, 1973

the grandson everything about his grandmother he wanted to remember, that one tape of her singing a single hymn could capture something as miraculous and complex as a beloved grandmother, a person he had lived so close to for so long, seemed to me profound and at the same time unlikely. How could one tape contain the essence, the totality of a person's life? Each of us is so large when we are alive, so full of breaths and emotions and attributes, we are all so precious and complex, how can all of that ever be reduced to several meters of magnetic plastic?

Over the next few days, I began to understand. The tape was so much more than a length of polymer, so much more than the words it contained. The tape was a container for June Marie Jones' voice, a vessel through which June Marie Jones could come alive for her family. Voice is the way we recognize from afar those we hold dear, when their image may be nothing but a blur, or when they are out of sight. Even during our lifetime, voice makes its way beyond our corporeal presence. A voice's vibrations, the softening or hardening of vowels, the liquidity of sibilants, all allow our ears — and perhaps other organs as well — to announce to us just who is speaking.

The telephone rings and we answer. If it is our spouse or partner, our mother or father, our child, our closest friend, a sister or brother, we need hear no more than "hello" to know — not just in our mind, but in our flesh and body as well — just who is on the other end of the line.

Despite being weak, the voice June Marie Jones' family knew and recognized from hearing her sing in church on Sundays rang out loud and clear for at least a measure or two on that tape, maybe more. Perhaps the middle C she reached with the words "sweet Jesus" replicated in its fullness the very voice that Sunday after Sunday rose from a wooden pew where LeAlan, his sister, and his mother, scrubbed clean and in their Sunday best, sat, all in a tidy row with June Marie Jones.

But there was even more of June Marie Jones on that several

meters of polymer tape than I at first realized. In addition to the actual physical voice, the notes, the vibrations, the tones and overtones, there was the song LeAlan's grandmother chose to sing. Because the Gospel felt real to her, had comforted her in times of sorrow, she chose a hymn to teach her grandson about her faith. June Marie Jones' decision to sing this particular hymn embodies the way this woman from the South Side of Chicago lived her life. Not a beseecher of miracles, of sudden healings, of overnight redemptions, June Marie Jones tells her grandson the essence of her faith as she sings:

> *I'm only human, I'm just a woman*
> *Help me believe in what I could be*
> *And all that I am*
> *Show me the stairway I have to climb*
> *Lord for my sake, help me to take*
> *One day at a time*

Within that voice surely echo conversations between grandmother and grandson, conversations when she told him he had a special name because of his uniqueness. When she assured him that, despite his mother's mental illness, she, his grandmother, would always be there to care for him. To love him. To encourage him. To believe in him.

Because it is a hymn she chose to sing, LeAlan can picture his grandmother in her church clothes: the broad-brimmed hats she probably wore, the box-shaped purse she might well have slipped between them on the pew, the jackets that reached below her hips with buttons glinting in the sunlight, and her high-heeled shoes. And as he listens to his grandmother sing on the tape, LeAlan might well sense her touch. The pitch and modulations of her voice might carry with them the warmth of her breath as she turned in the pew to speak to him about sitting still. Or the brush of her hand against his as she reached for the hymnal.

And hearing her voice surely takes him back to their house on Chicago's South Side, to the sofa where he slept each night, to his grandmother's room up a flight of rickety stairs. Then on to his grandfather dozing in his easy chair after a series of strokes. He would remember his grandmother feeding her once-carousing husband three meals a day with food that she prepared for the three grandchildren who lived with her as well.

The tape is like a magic lamp, storing within it the essence of a person and her life. From that tape, June Marie Jones materializes in all her incarnations: grandmother, mother, wife, churchgoer, disciplinarian, nurturer, pillar of the community, sufferer of tribulations here on earth, one of the Lord's blessed up in heaven. Each time he listens, his grandmother might come to him in a different form. Single notes might carry with them particular moments. Measures might release entire days.

Thinking about what LeAlan had said of the tape, I began to wonder what of each person I hold dear might serve the same purpose for me. Once my father is gone, will rereading his book be enough? Will the words on the page bring back his crooked finger, his impatience, his brilliance, his lust for adventure and travel, the cock of his head when he talks to babies? Could one of his paintings fully embody my husband, Stephen? His sweetness, his flights of fancy, his constant musing, his unruly beard, skinny legs, delicate wrists, the velvet of his voice? What qualities of my son, Jonah, would invoke his charm, his insistence on the priority of his goals, his impatience with anybody in his path, his generosity, his mop of curly hair, his tenderness?

But unable to settle on just what might be "enough" to bring back those I love, I became depressed. On that warm Sunday afternoon, driving across the Bay Bridge, I was thinking of loss and containment instead of life and expansion. I was thinking elimination and separation, not burgeoning and communion. Reduction and simplification rather than enlargement and complexity. Then I realized that what I had just engaged in was the opposite of LeAlan's "It would be enough." I was taking loved ones who are still living, and in their very aliveness incapable of containment, and attempting to contain them. Taking something wonderfully large and pulsing with life, and reducing it. And I was seeing that it couldn't be done, that the very essence of life is change and generation, growth and evolution. From one moment to the next, we are not exactly the same, and there I was trying to single out one quality of these people I love. To stop them in their tracks. To freeze them like pillars of salt.

Then I understood. I was not reclaiming all that I associate with a loved one from within a single cherished object. I was instead gathering all that I know and feel and sense about Jonah, about Stephen, and my father, and trying to force what is now twitching and pulsing with life into an inert container. I was seizing life and reducing it; while LeAlan, listening to several meters of magnetic plastic, his heart beating with love and admiration, was bringing the tape to life. With his grandmother no longer alive, focusing all of his attention on that one single tape was for him a form of resurrection. ▪

Finally Understanding Proust

I had just set out on a walk near Mendocino, Daphne trotting beside me, when a junco swooped down and alighted on an upper branch of a redbud tree growing just beyond the ditch on my left. I noted with pleasure the tiny bird's sooty black hood, its characteristic dark eyes, the sharp contrast between its head and the flesh color of its beak. When I paused to gaze more closely, the junco turned its head and spoke to me, a sharp *tick, tick, smack,* followed by a tittering trill. Then another, *tick, tick, smack.*

As I listened, everything became soft, the contours and boundaries of my body, the landscape around me, the physical world shimmering and elusive, like the stones in a kaleidoscope set in motion. When the stones stopped spinning and came to rest, their pattern momentarily fixed, they had deposited me on a tiny country lane in Iowa, near Kalona, not far from the one-room schoolhouse Mary Swander and I used as home base while we were traveling and conducting interviews for our book *Parsnips in the Snow.*

For several seconds I could feel the moist, heavy air of the Iowa summer, sense the swish of oat grass and goldenrod against my legs. All about me, the buzzing and clicking of insects and grasshoppers.

On either side, in the fields of our Amish neighbors, corn spiked toward the sky.

Along with the setting, the story behind how I happened to find myself on that tiny country lane unspooled in my mind's eye. My poet-friend, Mary, and I were in her Toyota pickup, driving away from the Amish country store to return to Iowa City, when we passed a schoolhouse on our right, up from the road and perched on a hill. We noticed the "For Rent" sign posted near the steps leading to the front door. But we did not stop. Instead, we continued driving, crossing a small bridge, the camper shell on Mary's truck rattling over the uneven paving. Then, something pulled me to turn and look back at the schoolhouse, growing smaller and smaller behind us.

"Mary, let's go back!"

We turned around, pulled up the driveway, and danced up the front steps. We peered through the small window in the front door. A bank of windows on the opposite side of a large room opened onto a sea of tall prairie grasses, and beyond that was a line of sky and trees. It was early afternoon, and the grasses waved in a gentle breeze.

"I'm feeling something like rapture of the deep," I told Mary.

"Me too," she replied.

Once we signed the rental contract, whenever we were not traveling to interview gardeners, we stayed at the schoolhouse, with its blue-tiled kitchen along the entry wall next to the front door, its sleeping loft, and its magnificent bank of windows. We quickly became acquainted with our Amish and Mennonite neighbors, who invited us into their fold to share dinner in their propane-fueled homes, to gather plump tomatoes and squash from their gardens, and to relax on their porches at night and listen to stories, the sky filled with the flash of lightening bugs.

One close neighbor dropped by at least once a day to stand in our doorway, his ragged gray beard brushing his chest as he offered the latest news about the crops, a shunning, a runaway teen, and always to poke fun at me for living in "crazy California."

At night, in the darkness, we listened to dogs howling, the trees and grasses hissing in the wind, the *clop, clop, clop* of horses' hooves drawing our neighbors' buggies by our house, their lanterns casting a line of light on our road.

When I emerged from my reverie, I realized that what had just swept over me was not like memory as I usually encounter it, a taste or smell taking me back to a particular time or experience in my past. Not like inhaling the aroma of onions, tomatoes, and beef, a rich ragout that reconnects me with my grandmother preparing Sunday dinner during one of my family's monthly visits to New York City. Not even like the experience of déjà vu that travels through the body, transporting its host back to one moment in the past.

This was memory, I realized, the way Proust first experienced it when he dipped his madeleine into his chamomile tea. Although I had studied Proust both as an undergraduate and graduate student, this morning, for the very first time, I understood the experience that infuses his seven-volume masterpiece. I understood not in a literary sense; his writing is too layered and complex ever to claim full literary mastery. No, this morning I understood Proust within my body, not my mind. This, despite the fact that for the past thirty years, I've thought I knew what he was writing about, how the madeleine brought back, in a rush of feeling, his past, embodied and integrated, not simply as memory but as experience. But until this morning, I knew and appreciated this intellectually only.

I understood Proust with my intellect because he evokes the moment of dipping the teacake into a cup of chamomile tea in exquisite detail. Because he writes, not of one memory but of an accumulation of memories: "I raised to my lips a spoonful of the tea in which I had soaked a morsel of the cake. No sooner had the warm liquid mixed with the crumbs touched my palate than a shudder ran through me and I stopped, intent upon the extraordinary thing that was happening to me. . . . The taste was that of the little piece of madeleine which on Sunday mornings at Combray (because on those mornings I did not go out before mass), when I went to say good morning to her in her bedroom, my aunt Léonie used to give me, dipping it first in her own cup of tea or tisane." Because he writes: "taste and smell alone, more fragile but more enduring, more unsubstantial, more persistent, more faithful, remain poised a long time, like souls, remembering, waiting, hoping, amid the ruins of all the rest; and bear unflinchingly, in the tiny and almost impalpable drop of their essence, the vast structure of recollection."[2]

Waking up from the reverie triggered by the junco, I realized that for years, I had mistaken Proust's evoking of this moment for the actual experience of such a moment; I had confused my visceral response to exquisite prose, to individual words and phrases perfectly strung together, with actually reliving the experience itself, a conflation all writers hope for — and few achieve.

The junco became my madeleine. And now, instead of thinking I know what Proust was writing about, I feel, on the most physical of levels, just what he felt when the taste of chamomile combined with a corner of the fluted pastry on his tongue. Not the taste of that particular combination, of course, but the wave of diffusion and disorientation that washed over him.

The dissolving of physical boundaries, of the here and now and the there and then, that I experienced that morning was not of me situated in a particular time and place, either in the present or the past. It was of me alive in a stretch of time that incorporated multiple moments and locations, a part of myself, the Iowa part, that engaged in behaviors and followed passions lost to me now.

In Iowa one day, out for a solo drive in the country, I sat for an hour, my car pulled to the side of a lane, following a family of red-headed woodpeckers as they swooped from one maple tree at the edge of a barnyard to another tree at the perimeter of the field across the way. For the entire hour, what mattered to me was not

2. Marcel Proust, *Remembrance of Things Past*, Vol I: *Swann's Way*. Translated into English in 1922.

the act of observing — I was not hoping to discover anything I didn't know about the behavior or the song of these birds — but the simple pleasure I took in watching. I didn't ask myself what the woodpeckers were about. What their behavior meant or involved. I didn't try to understand what I saw. Spending an hour in this way, satisfying my pleasure at the birds in flight, was an indulgence of the sort I habitually denied myself. But in Iowa, somehow, the usual strictures and conventions of my life, the need for constant gainful employment, the necessity of shaping and benefiting in a concrete way from every situation dissolved.

In Iowa, I looked forward to raking the leaves from the two giant apple trees that towered over all other vegetation in the backyard of the house we were renting on Summit Street while I attended the Writers' Workshop. Before and after Iowa, leaf raking was a chore. It hurt my back and drew blisters on my hands. But in Iowa, I raked for hours, enjoying the scrape of the rake tines as they etched hundreds of tiny canals all over the lawn, looking up from time to time to admire our neighbor's tulip tree, still clinging to its once-bright-green leaves now turned yellow; or to inhale the fall air, crisp with a hint of winter.

It has been years since I've returned to Iowa, and sadly, my Iowa friends have largely disappeared from my life. A divorce and a second marriage, along with work have kept me away. But I still carry Iowa and the schoolhouse within me; its smells and tastes have permeated my cells, to combine with the blood that pulses through my heart and keeps me alive. And I still miss Iowa, no less now than the first summer I stayed away. I miss the corn spiking in the fields in August, the rich loam of Iowa gardens, the stories neighbors told, never in a hurry to reach the climax. I miss the work Mary and I did together. I miss Mary.

This morning, thanks to one tiny bird, Iowa was returned to me. Not just one place. Not a single moment. Not a particular person or an isolated day. But an entire cast of characters, and with them the joy of at least ten years of my life. ▪

Our Best Asset

Two days after returning from a trip to Brazil, I was walloped by a 103-degree fever. Three days later, when the fever hadn't budged, I went to see my doctor, who suspected I had come down with a case of Dengue Fever, a tropical disease spread by mosquitoes. There's not much to be done for Dengue, aside from hydration and frequent blood tests to make certain platelet counts don't dip dangerously low. So my doctor sent me home with instructions to get lots of rest, to stay away from public places, and to return to the lab to have my blood drawn for each of the next four days.

The following afternoon when I arrived at the lab, patients overflowed the large waiting room, many dozing in their seats, others slouched against walls. One of the receptionists had gone home sick an hour earlier, and a replacement hadn't yet arrived. I dropped my membership card into the slot at the front desk, then found a free bit of wall at one end of the room, where I leaned back, closed my eyes, and wondered if I'd be able to stay awake until a chair became available. One of the symptoms of Dengue Fever, in addition to pain, is extreme fatigue.

Before I closed my eyes, I noticed a beautiful Asian woman

several feet from me, feeding a little girl who sat in a stroller. Each time I opened my eyes to scan the room for the seat I so desperately wanted, I was drawn to what at first appeared to be this quintessential mother-child scene. Feeling feverish and achy as I did, I found watching a young mother nourish her child soothing, dipping the spoon into the plastic bowl, then tenderly slipping it into her child's mouth. Again and again. Dip, slip, dip, slip.

Slowly, though, I realized that something about the scene was unusual. That wasn't a spoon the mother held, but a tiny syringe. And she wasn't positioning it in the front of her child's mouth; she was inserting it into the side and working it to the back of the little girl's tongue. Then I looked more closely at the child: she was at least three years old, of an age to feed herself!

Something was wrong here! With that realization, a shot of adrenaline coursed through me. This child could not eat on her own! In fact, she didn't seem to understand the act of eating or the significance of food. She never moved her hands toward her mouth; they remained inertly at her sides. Nor did she open her mouth in anticipation of the syringe. She didn't even seem to register its contents. And instead of focusing on her mother, she gazed intently at something that had caught her interest across the room.

Overwhelmed by the rush of adrenaline, my fatigue vanished. This poor beautiful mother. How she must suffer for her child.

When I was pregnant with Jonah, I maintained a constant state of anxiety about everything. I might miscarry, or I could develop toxemia, as my sister-in-law had. The cord could be wrapped around my baby's neck, depriving him of oxygen at birth. At the very least, my baby might be missing a finger or toe. And later? My child could be autistic. Become a drug addict like my brother. Or suffer from serious clinical depression like two of my uncles.

When the nurse handed me my perfect baby boy at 2:17 A.M. one July 5, his eyes wide and gazing directly into mine, my first reaction was incredulity. "You mean there's nothing wrong with him!" I exclaimed.

Busy stitching my episiotomy, the obstetrician looked up. "In all my years of delivering babies, I've never encountered a mother so worried that something would go wrong."

As it was, even with my perfect baby, I found cause to worry. He was a barracuda of a nurser, five minutes and he'd had enough. Even though my pediatrician assured me that Jonah was getting more than sufficient nourishment, I fretted about his potential to bond. While other newborns and their mothers passed blissful hours, the baby suckling, the mother gazing down adoringly, Jonah and I established no such relaxed intimacy. What did this mean for his future relationships? Would he ever have friends? Fall in love?

And when at five months, he began propelling himself around with his arms, his legs dragging behind him, I worried that he might never actually crawl, which I'd read was essential for the development of certain areas of his brain. Should I work on patterning him to crawl? Should I consult a specialist?

"Oh, Stephanie, you've had enough! You don't want any more." The mother's soft voice brought me back to the waiting room. "O. K., you don't have to eat any more," Stephanie's mother assured her, as she wiped Stephanie's mouth and handed her a tiny rubber giraffe, which Stephanie plucked from her mother's hand, then let fall onto the floor. "Here you are, Stephanie," the mother said. "You love your little giraffe; don't you want to play with it?"

Stephanie glanced at the toy her mother held up for her, then looked away, toward where I was standing. When our eyes met, I smiled, but she turned her head.

"Oh, Stephanie, you're usually friendly. Don't you want to say hello?" her mother asked. But Stephanie only buried her head further into the back of her stroller.

When I next opened my eyes, Stephanie's mother was busy

with Stephanie again, now inserting a large, white-plastic syringe into Stephanie's abdomen. As she pushed the plunger down, she tenderly brushed hair from Stephanie's eyes. Again and again, she filled the syringe, inserted it, and plunged the nourishment into Stephanie's stomach. I looked at my watch. I had been standing there for forty-five minutes, the mother feeding her daughter the whole while.

If Stephanie were my child, I wondered, how would I function? Not with the poise and serenity of this woman, seemingly unaware of the crowd in the waiting room. I would be self-conscious, awkward, resentful of the stares I could feel searing my back. I might even feel humiliated at my failure to produce a healthy child. Yet watching this mother tend to Stephanie, I realized that, for her, nobody else existed. Not the patients dozing in their seats, nor those leaning against the walls. Not the children whining next to their mothers, forced to "sit still" longer than they could bear. Not the tiny girl running back and forth between where her mother sat and the wall, her ringlets bouncing. In the midst of the crowded waiting room, this young mother had created a private zone around her child and herself, a space of love and tenderness, of pure devotion. And despite the inherent awkwardness of the situation, she fulfilled her role with grace, her attention locked on her child, her movements assured and fluid.

"Jane Anne Staw." I heard my name and went to the front desk to register. When I was finished, I saw that a seat had opened up next to Stephanie and her mother. The feeding was over, and the young mother was packing up all her equipment into the three bags hanging over the back of the stroller. As I sat down, I decided to engage with this mother and not pretend that everything was normal. A friend who went through eight months of chemotherapy taught me compassionate honesty when she explained that she welcomed appropriate comments about her baldness. "After all, there was clearly something wrong, and I felt touched if people acknowledged that in a caring way," she told me.

"You sure have to travel heavy, don't you?" I ventured.

"Yes, it takes a lot to feed Stephanie. But she's our miracle baby," the mother smiled.

"Miracle baby?"

"She was born with all her organs in her chest. It took three months to sort things out." The mother was still smiling.

"That must have been so hard for you," I said.

"Stephanie's the one it was hard for. She has had twenty operations."

"She is indeed a miracle," I replied.

"Now I feed her only four times a day. But in the beginning, we were up throughout the night.

I smiled at Stephanie, who again turned away.

"She's usually very friendly," her mother apologized. "I don't know what's happening today. Stephanie, don't you want to say hello?"

"Will she be able to feed herself someday?" I couldn't help but ask, suddenly worried for both Stephanie and her mother. What would it be like to know you were tethered to your child for a lifetime of feeding? Not just feeding, but injecting her with nourishment? Four times a day. Day after day. The room felt close, the air around me dense.

"She might be able to feed herself one day. She might even be able to do it now, but I can't rush her," Stephanie's mother offered. "We have to move according to Stephanie's timetable."

I thought about this child, who after several years was still completely dependent upon her mother; and I thought about this young mother, tied so fully to her daughter. How small the mother's universe had necessarily become. Before her baby was born, this mother might have worked, moved freely about in the world. She might have attended concerts, pedaled her bike

SMALL: THE LITTLE WE NEED FOR HAPPINESS

into the hills, met friends for lunch from time to time, her gaze directed outward, widening to encompass friends and family, work and passions, their contrails connecting her with other cities, other countries, other lives. Now, instead, her vision had to be circumscribed nearly to a pinpoint, everything focused upon her child. There wasn't time to roam or wander.

"Stephanie Wilson," the receptionist called.

"That's us," the mother said. Then, "Stephanie, don't you want to say goodbye?"

I smiled and waved, but once again, Stephanie twisted in her stroller, turning her head from me.

"I don't know why she's being so shy, today," the mother said. "She's usually very social. It's one of her best assets." Then she wheeled Stephanie into the drawing room.

As I watched them disappear, "one of her best assets" echoed in my head. Suddenly, I felt a sense of gratitude toward that beautiful young mother who, despite her child's extreme disability, appreciated and applauded a unique quality in her daughter. Focusing on a single attribute, loving and nurturing Stephanie in the waiting room of Kaiser's lab, the young woman had allowed me to share in the glow she projected for her miracle baby. As Stephanie and her mother vanished from sight around a corner, I understood that I had been wrong. Stephanie hadn't caused her mother's world to shrink. Not at all. Nurturing Stephanie, focusing uniquely on Stephanie, the mother and her vision had grown larger, much larger — large enough to discover the grace in it all. ∎

The Serengeti Plain

My husband, Stephen, and I have taken to walking along the shore of the Navarro River on Sunday mornings when we're up in the Anderson Valley. We wake up early, have a cup of tea, then hop in the car and drive the ten minutes to Hendy Woods, winding through the park with its lush, old-growth redwood groves, until we arrive at the parking lot by the meadow, where we disembark. The river is on the other side of the meadow, down an embankment, its wide shores paved with river rocks.

It was the rocks that drew Stephen to the river and its shores. He remembered them from family outings years ago and wanted to revisit a favorite haunt. While at first I was more captivated by the life along the river — the egrets and belted kingfishers, the river otters and great blue herons — the spirit of the hunt quickly captured me. Sunday mornings found the two of us, several feet apart, walking slowly, hunched over, heads down, peering at the ground, each eager to show the other our finds. It wasn't the predictable river rocks that rewarded us, although their smooth, gray egg-shapes are indeed lovely, but the hidden jade or pale coral specimens. "Oh, look at this one," each of us would call to the other periodically. "Do we have one like this?"

It was quite a companionable pursuit, and we appeared to have settled into an intimate and predictable routine. Then one Sunday morning in March, I noticed, peeking up among what seemed at first an endless expanse of rocks, several of the most delicate of green blades. I bent down to get a closer look. They were pristine: perfectly formed, flattened, green plant tissue, about three inches long, tinged with red along the edge. *How in the world had they found their way through the rocks? And how was it that they were not bruised in the process?*

I walked on a ways and came upon several more exquisite blades, moist with dew, nearly translucent in the morning light. As I continued, I discovered other plants poking up among the rocks, some with tube-shaped leaves, others vine-like, yet others formed into miniature rosettes, each coming forth in isolation, a separate universe, far from any other sign of burgeoning plant life along the river's rocky shore. I quickly found myself moved to tears by these first tiny thrusts of new life among the rocks. "Oh, you poor sweet things," I wanted to cry out, "you've found an opening and pushed yourself up into light, into life. You are brave survivors."

I began photographing these diminutive plants, working to achieve the proper perspective, one that would capture at the same time their fragility and the surrounding rockscape. It was a delicate balance: zooming in rendered the plants larger than life but captured their delicacy; panning out incorporated the desert of rocks while eclipsing the details of the tender shoots. The dilemma was both aesthetic and emotional. I wanted to capture the perfection of the plants, but it was a tenuous perfection, intensified by the surrounding landscape of rock. I wasn't moved by the beauty of these emerging flora alone; it was the context of this beauty that had me hooked.

For the past twenty-five years I have taught literary nonfiction writing. I have worked with undergraduates at Stanford, master's candidates at the University of Iowa and the University of San

Francisco, and extension students at the University of California, Berkeley. But no matter where I teach, I have consistently remarked on the number of students in my classes who were neglected or abused as children. When the first student wrote of years of beatings at his parents' hands, I felt shocked and horrified. When the first woman described her father's sexual molestation of her, I felt outraged. Over the years, my shock and horror and outrage have transmuted into admiration and marvel and appreciation for the survivors.

I am a person within whom each emotional event, no matter how apparently small, resonates intensely. Delightful when the event is joyous, this reactivity becomes nearly crippling when I am criticized or chastised. To survive, I learned to make no waves. I was the good girl, the model child, the perfect citizen. And even then, I suffered. How would I have survived continued beatings, to say nothing of sexual violation?

Yet all of my students have survived. Indeed, quite a few have done much more. They have flourished, completing undergraduate degrees with honors and continuing on to graduate school. Not surprisingly, their childhood abuse or their chaotic nuclear families became the subject many of them write about. But for me, that is beside the point. What I find remarkable is that any of them made it out of the jungle of their childhood at all. How in the world did they escape?

I've received some clues recently from the series *Planet Earth*. My stepson, Nathan, bought the DVDs for us, and each night, once we've finished our work and chores, Stephen and I settle down to journey to the bottom of the seas or to the peaks of the earth's tallest mountains. Each night I am struck anew by the simultaneous beauty and cruelty of our universe. No sooner do we admire an aerial view of the Serengeti Plain, with its vast dun-colored grasslands dolloped with the green of acacias, all blanketed by the clear blue of the sky overhead, than we witness a pride of lions closing in on a baby elephant or an eagle swooping down on an African rabbit. At first I thought the series editors might be responsible for this constant juxtaposition of splendor and violence, but I have come to understand that it is not bias but truth they are filming. And it is only because they are able to see from multiple perspectives, both up close and from afar, that they capture again and again the collision of these contrasts.

This is life, the editors are demonstrating, full of exquisite beauty and horrific violence. What is more, life goes on. Despite its frequent births and deaths, droughts and famines, seemingly endless migrations, and the constant threat of natural predators, life on the Serengeti Plain endures, season after season, year after year, decade after decade. More than about death and dying, life on this earth is about survival. We have known this ever since Darwin wrote his *On the Origin of Species,* and I have read all about it of late in the works of evolutionary biologists. But if I had known about survival, it remained an abstraction to me, the subject of experiments, a theory for scientists to discuss and dispute. I had never thought of it as something I witness each day in my most ordinary of lives.

Until, that is, I became absorbed in the tiny plants pushing their way through the rocks on the shores of the Navarro River. If at first I thought I understood my attraction to these brave little flora, my understanding has deepened over the past seven months as I have continued to photograph and watch them mature. What I have come to understand is that despite their apparent fragility, each of the plants has one resilient feature. For some, it is a sturdy stem, for others it is the fleshiness of the leaves that resists bruising, with yet others it is suppleness and flexibility. Each possesses one particular asset that assists them in the struggle for survival.

I think back to the hunter and prey relationships captured in the *Planet Earth* series. There too, the contest is balanced by the strength particular to each species: the wolf possesses endurance, but the caribou has speed; size and power are on the side of the elephant, but the lion works by cunning; the advantage of the desert eagle is in flight, the hare's advantage is camouflage.

The same must be true of my students who have survived hardship, neglect, and abuse at the hands of their parents or siblings. Be it defiance, stubbornness, wiliness, toughness, persistence, or charm, they each have a gift their siblings, many of whom spiral into alcoholism and drug addiction, lack. Thanks to their particular gift, these students, though they have suffered and bear the scars of their wounds, survive. They are able to absorb from their environment the nourishment they need to push upward toward the light.

Even I, I now realize, have found my way up between the rocks. Although I didn't suffer the violence of many of my students, I grew up in my own version of a rocky landscape. My father, a brilliant scientist, was impatient and could brook no flaws — neither in thinking nor behavior. Anxiety pummeled my mother's life; she never learned to drive and hardly ventured out on her own. While I became a yogi and learned to hold my breath, my brother turned to drugs. Thinking about my family of origin, I can recognize the asset that helped me survive. I was able to do as I was told, to weigh each word and action for its consequences, to hold my tongue. I could think ahead. My brother, full of passion and restlessness, could not.

The tiny plants along the shores of the Navarro River have taught me all of this. They are my newest and unlikeliest teachers. Despite their size, from the moment they first thrust themselves up between the river rocks, they hold within them some of the world's greatest truths. ■

TINY HOUSES

Not long ago, a client brought a book called *Tiny Houses* to her appointment. She had just bought land near Mendocino, California, and was gathering ideas for a cabin she might build there. My client, a tiny fine-boned woman, so thin that her mother worried about her weight the whole time she was growing up, was thrilled at the prospect of creating a small space for herself, miles off the main road, in a clearing just outside a grove of fir trees. "Just think," she told me, "everything inside will be within arm's reach."

The houses pictured in the book were indeed perfect miniatures, designed and constructed with loving attention and care. Yet turning the pages of her book, I experienced a rush of claustrophobia. Everything within sight, no rooms to wander off into. Although I've always loved small spaces, looking at the photos with my client, I felt myself panicking, overcome with claustrophobia at the thought of living in such a circumscribed area, no matter how exquisite and perfectly engineered.

Years earlier, as an MRI technician slid the gurney I was lying on into what looked to me like a high-tech casket, I had reacted in the same way. Once my shoulders slipped through the opening, with only my neck and head outside imminent confinement, a surge of panic raced through me. "Stop," I wanted to shout. "Please, please, don't push me in the rest of the way! I'll die." But instead of crying out, I closed my eyes and visualized a meadow in my favorite wilderness area, a blue dome of sky overhead, stands of nodding wildflowers and grasses all around me, and my panic gradually subsided.

While my reaction to the confinement of the MRI seemed reasonable — indeed it is quite common — this recent outbreak of claustrophobia in response to my client's book took me by surprise. Unlike many of my friends who yearn for vast vistas atop mountains, I'm happiest peeking through a break in the trees to the California hills in the distance, above them a slice of sky. In wide-open spaces, I feel lost, abandoned to the elements. When I lived in the Midwest, unless I imagined myself safely ensconced in a wagon train of pioneers, the expansiveness of the Great Plains appeared menacing to me. In fact, tucked into a wagon rolling across vast expanses of prairie might have been a perfect situation for me: cozily embraced within a panoramic setting. Perhaps that is why visualizing a meadow while encased in an MRI tunnel dispelled my claustrophobia. The combination of smallness surrounding and embracing me, alongside an opening onto the larger world is my Golden Mean.

My discomfort with open space may well be a result of my poor sense of direction. North, south, east, and west are abstractions that mean nothing to me, unless I can link them to local and familiar landmarks. When I travel to San Francisco from my home in Berkeley, I know I am headed west only by visualizing the Bay Bridge on one side of the city and the ocean far across on the other side. Sometimes even this act of visualization is not enough. To find my way after a wrong turn in San Francisco, I have to pull over to the curb and, in my mind's eye, place myself with my back to the Bay Bridge and my face toward the ocean, before I can decide whether to head to the left or right. Unlike Stephen, I have never been able to find my bearings by looking at the position of the sun or the constellations in the sky.

I am easily overwhelmed visually. Looking at a painting for the first time, I must take several minutes to focus before I can really see what's in front of me. Colors, objects, strokes, shading, all clamor for my attention simultaneously, dizzying me so that I cannot assemble the various elements into a whole. That might be why I find the wagon train image a solace; it provides me with a point of reference without which my eyes would otherwise not know where to rest. Viewing a landscape, I scan what is before my eyes randomly, taking in everything at once, unable to find a comfortable moment of stillness so that I may bring what I observe into focus.

For these reasons, I have always found small spaces embracing rather than confining. Given an alcove off a grand room or a modest garden tucked in the corner of an acreage, I am not afraid of getting lost or overwhelmed, and am content to look from my cozy alcove across the open space toward the grand piano, or with a flowerbed at my side, to squint and bring a distant barn into focus.

So why the wave of claustrophobia looking at the small houses pictured in my client's book? Why, sitting in my sunny garden office, turning the pages of a beautiful edition, where every board and nail, each corner and opening is fully intentional, did I suddenly feel as if someone were sitting on my chest, cutting off my next breath?

Reflecting on my reaction, I realized that small spaces have always symbolized solace when I face vastness and expanse: vistas of open land, mountain ranges, or oceans, as well as a life packed with too many people, events, and demands. It is always in these situations of largeness that I seek out a small safe place for retreat. How different that is from a dramatically limited life space, within which I would have little choice of which way to turn.

Not long after my experience with the book of tiny houses, I was visiting some friends who own land in the country. Taking a walk early one morning, we passed a tiny A-frame, set back from the road. "Does anybody live there?" I asked.

"It was empty for a while, but a middle-aged woman has been living there for the past six months."

At my friend's response, I found myself experiencing the same rush of panic that had seized me as I paged through the book on tiny houses. "What does she do during the rainy season?" I asked.

"What do you mean?" my friend looked at me quizzically.

By this time, we had arrived back at my friend's house, and I let the conversation drop. But I realized that the explanation I had concocted for my reaction to my client's book was only partly true. Something deeper was at work here. But what? What had changed for me? When once I had been drawn to tiny spaces, why now did the prospect of living small feel so unbearable to me? Why did it send me into a full-blown panic?

Is it possible that my reaction of panic was the consequence of an early childhood experience just now coming to the fore? Reading up on claustrophobia, I learned that some psychologists look as far back as early childhood or even the birth experience for clues to their clients' fears. Was I ever locked in a closet? Did my younger brother once put a pillow over my head and try to suffocate me? Or was my birth particularly traumatic? Did I get caught in my mother's birth canal? Was the umbilical cord wrapped around my neck, preventing me from taking my first breath?

Or is the shift I seem to be experiencing physiological rather than psychological? Does it have something to do with the slowing down of my metabolism? Or the increasing inefficiency of my synapses? Perhaps I used to think more quickly and more globally, my mind racing far ahead of the time and place where I was situated. With my brain no longer speeding along, perhaps I feel small spaces as confining or trapped, with slim possibility of escape.

My reaction may well have to do with age. When I was younger and life felt like an infinite unknown, a vast future full of emotions and people, places, and events I could not even begin to fathom, the temporary constraint of space served perhaps as a resting place, where I could float quietly and serenely, without being pulled out into the sea of the rest of my life. Now that I am older, with more than half of my life trailing behind me and my future reduced, living small might be a material manifestation of my prospects. A tiny dwelling becomes a confrontation of the limits my age imposes upon me.

Several of my friends have recently become acutely aware of their mortality. Every new experience, every moment of joy is tinged for them with regret for all the time that has passed and the reduced time that remains. While I haven't been aware of this reaction to aging within myself, perhaps my newly-acquired claustrophobia is an expression of this regret.

I had been reflecting on all of this for several days, when a photographer I recently met told me about the five years he had spent teaching blind students to take photographs. "Tell me something is impossible and I do just the opposite," he quipped.

"And how did the project turn out?" I asked.

"The students learned about so much more than picture taking," he said. "They learned about telling stories, they learned what they cared about, they learned how to take responsibility for their camera, they learned about undertaking and completing a project. And more important than any of this, they learned that they were capable of so much more than most people thought."

Intrigued, I asked him what other impossible projects he had pulled off.

"When I was in graduate school," he began laughing, "my dorm room was so small that when I got out of bed in the morning, I bumped into the wall. I mean this room was ridiculously small. So what did I do? I decided to have a dinner party. I took the mattress off the bed and replaced it with a board. Then I invited ten friends for dinner. The only requirement was that each person tell a story about small. So we sat in my room, our feet tucked under the bed, ate a delicious meal and told stories."

"I think you've just saved me," I told my new friend.

"Saved you?"

I explained that I was struggling with recently-acquired claustrophobia. In the past, I relished small spaces and would probably have felt quite comfortable in his tiny dorm room. But now, even the thought of being spatially confined caused me to panic. "But you've given me a kind of visual mantra," I told him. "From now on, each time I begin to feel my pulse quickening, I will conjure the image of your dinner party in your tiny dorm room, everybody sitting around your bed telling stories."

More than a visual mantra, my friend's story has served to guide me into seeing additional possibilities of small. Instead of an impossibly tiny dorm room, I see a group of friends, shoulders and thighs touching, gathered from all over the university campus and town where they live, to share a meal. And I see them telling stories that transcend time and place, each tale unique, yet together creating a tapestry of this evening they are spending with one another, talking and laughing in the tiny dorm room. Through this image, what was once a minuscule space expands to include not only the photographer's friends assembled on that one evening, but those times they will encounter each other in the future as well, when they will again gather or meet, by happenstance or by arrangement, several of them or all of them as a group.

And there is still more. The room for me is not simply the photographer's friends who have gathered in the dorm room, but the friends and families his friends carry with them, those dear ones in their thoughts that day, or who will come to mind the next day, all those who have contributed to making the ten friends gathered for dinner who they are. All those who, in their hearts and in their spirits, hold these friends dear as they go about their own lives, all over the country and perhaps all over the world.

From a tiny space whose square footage was consumed by a bed, my photographer's dorm room expanded into the multiple lives of a whole world, an entire universe even. From now on, whenever I feel the initial tingles of claustrophobia, I will visualize that scene, confident that the space I inhabit, no matter how small, will expand into a place of comfort and possibility. ▪

CRANBERRY SAUCE

DON'T WAIT. ORDER YOUR THANKSGIVING WILLIE BIRD Now!

As soon as I caught sight of the banner fluttering over the entrance to my local poultry shop — a full month before Thanksgiving — my stomach tightened. Thanksgiving is my annual proving ground, the one holiday when all the expectations, anticipations, and traditions of my culture, to say nothing of family and friends, flood my psyche. Newspapers displaying color photos of exquisite meals, along with recipes — both tried-and-true dishes and suggestions for delectable innovation — taunt me weeks before that celebrated Thursday in November. *Try brining your turkey this year. What about a polenta dressing? If you want a perfect turkey, make this the year of the sure-fire slow-roast method.* In the local markets, displays and conversations converge to heighten anticipation. *I made the best turkey ever last year by basting it every ten minutes. I swear by low temperature roasting. All my guests tell me my turkey is the best they've ever tasted. Here's what I do . . . .*

I have never questioned the expectations that surround this holiday; instead I have internalized them as my own. I've never served fewer than seven dishes. I prepare everything from scratch. And I admit I've taken to brining the turkey as well. I do all this while feeling overwhelmed by the idea of producing a holiday meal for guests who will measure my food against their own Thanksgiving standards, often established by generations of women in their families. There's no doubt in my mind that what graces my table will be under scrutiny. Weeks before the actual meal, my head swirls with potential criticisms. *My mother's stuffing is tastier. I prefer the crust in my aunt's pie. My grandmother's turkey was never this dry.* In addition, I have my own perfectionism to raise the stakes. Toward the beginning of November each year, a paragon chef takes residence in my head and fills me with doubt about not only the finished products, but my process of creating them as well. I can never seem to execute the strokes required to mince so that all the action is in my wrist. Nor have I mastered the process of caramelizing onions, which requires just the right amount of even heat and stirring to avoid charring the delicate translucent slices.

As the date looms closer, the tension rises, so that getting the Thanksgiving meal on the table has always meant several days of hand wringing. To say nothing of worrying about just when to shop: not so early that I overload for too many days the capacity of my kitchen, and not so late that I have to battle all the last-minute holiday chefs. Once I've made the shopping decision, and I've gathered all the components of the meal, my kitchen is transformed into my version of the Indy 500, including crash sites. I sauté onions for the stuffing, while at the same time rinse and cull the cranberries for the sauce, roast the pecans for the stuffing, and attempt, "one last time," to roll out a decent pie crust. Fifteen minutes later, I mince fresh sage, grate orange zest, and wipe up the flour I spilled when my elbow bumped the canister as I rushed to prevent the onions from burning.

This year, to modulate the stress and strain, I challenged myself to enjoy my Thanksgiving preparations and to find a way to extract the frenzy and self-flagellation from the process. I arranged my schedule so that I could shop three full days in advance. And I decided to begin cooking three nights ahead of time, promising myself that I would not cram too much into each night in the kitchen. And, since I had recently vowed to "think small," I decided I would spend the first night focusing on the cranberry sauce. That and nothing more. A rinse and culling of the berries, then into a saucepan, along with orange zest and juice, freshly-grated ginger, honey, and pecan bits — that was all it would take to create a glistening ruby mound of berries. No mincing and grating, sifting and whipping, no butter scorching or sink filling with measuring spoons and cups, greasy pans, and caked knives. Just berries, plain and simple.

As I emptied the bag of cranberries into my colander, I found myself beginning to relax. Devoting the entire evening to preparing this one simple dish was a luxury I had never indulged in before, and suddenly it seemed as if time were slowing down. Instead of running at *allegrissimo* speed, I was living at *larghissimo*, where every note and each pause called attention to themselves. When about half the cranberries had fallen from the bag, I became acutely aware of their *plink, plink, plink* as they tumbled into the metal colander. *Plink, plink, plink*, a shower of cranberries, I thought, and was transported to the shores of a mountain lake, listening to a summer's rain striking the metal roof of a cabin.

All of my senses were heightened. For the first time since I'd been preparing Thanksgiving, I noticed the shapes of the berries, which ranged from perfectly round to oval. I also took in their palette of hues: ruby and rose, pink and burgundy, each berry a unique combination of color and shape; the overhead kitchen fixture reflected, in a pinprick of light, on every single surface, a galaxy of cranberry stars in my sink. And instead of rushing, I was moving at half-time, my hands floating down to the counter, my feet crossing the maple floor in languorous glissades.

Once before, though under very different circumstances, I had a similar experience of time slowing down. Crossing the Bay Bridge one Sunday afternoon, I noticed how little traffic there was. Right on the heels of that observation, I spotted a pickup and a sedan in two different lanes just ahead of me, traveling about fifty miles an hour toward the same lane. *OH*, I remember thinking, *I BETTER GET OUT OF THE WAY. THEY'RE GOING TO CRASH AND I DON'T WANT TO PLOW INTO THEM.*

As I considered changing lanes, I wondered why my brain had turned to molasses, for it seemed to me that I was thinking very, very slowly. *CHANGE LANES*, my brain was telling me, as if each thought that formed in my head and each word that made itself heard were bubbling up from deep within the sea. *GOSH*, I thought, *I'D BETTER MOVE FASTER OR I'M GOING TO GET CAUGHT IN THE MIDDLE!*

Despite my sluggish thoughts, I did manage to maneuver myself out of harm's way that afternoon. But later, as I pulled off the freeway to catch my breath, I was disturbed by how very slowly I seemed to react. It was only a miracle, I thought, that I had escaped being part of such a terrible collision. Once I gathered my wits about me, I realized that the molasses experience must have been an illusion. If I had actually responded as slowly as it felt, I would have been smashed right between the truck and car that collided.

Later, I discovered that I was not alone in experiencing time warp in a crisis or high-impact situation. In baseball, for example, successful batters often describe the pitched ball both as coming toward them in slow motion and appearing to be as large as a grapefruit. Although the neurological mechanisms involved in these processes are not yet understood, it seems clear that our brains take advantage of the fluidity of time and space when we are in danger or in other situations where our reaction time is critical.

As I prepared the cranberry sauce, however, it wasn't a crisis that triggered the deceleration of time. This time, the seconds slowed because I had deliberately altered the rhythms of my habitual actions. Ask any of my friends or family and they'll tell you that when I cook, I seem to be in a race against myself. "What's the hurry?" my mother used to ask whenever she watched me prepare a meal. And if hurry was my ordinary kitchen tempo, imagine me around Thanksgiving, when I was feeling unusually pressured. This year, by streamlining my Thanksgiving preparations, instead of flight-or-fight messages, I was transmitting stay-and-savor impulses to my cerebral cortex.

Slowly, over the next days, I began to understand the common thread among preparing cranberry sauce, a near-traffic accident, and baseball batting. Decelerating the pace of my cooking, focusing on one preparation, one single ingredient at a time, I was no longer consumed with my usual anxiety about the results. For the first time, my performance no longer mattered. It was the cranberries that counted, not me and my cooking expertise. In the case of the freeway incident, while my performance was indeed at stake, it was my life that was on the line, not my ego. No time or space for second guessing, for doubt, for my habitual perseveration. My thoughts and decisions and I were one, experiencing a rare convergence of focus.

I imagine that something similar takes place for the batter experiencing an expansion of time and space, standing at the plate, waiting for the pitcher to release the ball. On those occasions, the ball, not the player's performance, claims the center of the batter's attention. The crowds, the rest of the team, the coach, the pitcher, even the body of the batter must disappear from sight and perception, while all senses concentrate on the white globe arcing from the hand of the pitcher toward the bat.

So what changed? What was behind the drop in my anxiety and worry about performance? In these situations, the ego disappeared, the ego being that part of the self that intrudes too frequently in our lives, creating the schisms, the divisions we often refer to as the voices in our heads. *Do this. No, do that. Pay attention. Be careful. Remember the last time you struck out. Don't add too much sugar. The sauce is going to be sour. Everyone will hate it.* These voices stopped, and that has made all the difference.

By the time my cranberry sauce was cooling in my favorite Delft blue ceramic dish, I had experienced a High Mass of sound, smell, color, texture, and taste: the popping of the berries as they simmered, the translucence of the orange zest once it was heated through, the cloud of steam hovering above the saucepan, the prickle of sourness in the air, the frothing, burbling, sucking as the concoction simmered on the stove, and the final glistening and deepening of color as it cooled in the bowl.

The cranberry sauce, that one tiny part of the entire Thanksgiving meal, became a celebration of all that is most profound in the acts of cooking and communion. Once the sauce was cooling, whenever I glanced over at the sparkling red mound, I was reminded of the process of its preparation: the washing of the berries, the culling, the heating and purifying, the communion with orange zest and pecans. All of this, each and every rinse and stir, addition and tasting, moved me that much closer to the final celebration, three days later, when all those tiny steps would converge the moment my family and guests congregated around my dining room table to enjoy together the holiday meal I had prepared for them. ▪

Ten-to-the-Minus-Twenty-Eighth of a Second

T IME RARELY SEEMS TO BE ON MY SIDE. EITHER IT WHIZZES by and I find myself rushing — to finish preparing dinner, to get out the door for an appointment, to weed my perennial bed before my guests arrive — or time drags, such that a free morning or afternoon feels endless and my life a void. When I find myself in this latter relationship with time, I have nothing, absolutely nothing to do. Nothing to fill the hours ahead, nothing to coax me out of the chair I am sitting on and move me into the future.

Thankfully, I haven't experienced this crushing weight of time in quite a while. That was more an experience of my youth and early adulthood. When in elementary school or junior high, I remember walking in my neighborhood on a mid-summer's day, seeing no one on our suburban Philadelphia block, experiencing the stillness, heaviness, and silence of the humid July air and sensing the vacuum of the rest of the summer lower itself onto me. Or later, when in Paris as a college junior, my French family away for the weekend, *samedi* and *dimanche* often yawned in my face, presenting no prospects for filling the hours until Monsieur and Madame Pautrat and their daughter Delphine returned, and it would once again be time for me to attend classes at the Sorbonne.

What did I do to pass the time over these endless weekends? I honestly can't remember. Did I take long walks? Read? Go to the movies? I must have done something. I don't think I spent entire days huddled up in my tiny room in the apartment on Avenue Pierre Premier de Serbie. But from this distance I can't be sure; either this all happened too long ago, or it is simply too painful to recall.

For quite a while, whenever I remembered those bleak Parisian weekends, I felt ashamed. How in the world could I have found myself marooned in Paris, of all places? What a poor specimen of a human being I was. What was wrong with me? Now I see that there was, indeed, something wrong: I was struggling with depression, a master at bleeding all color from the world and inflating time until even a single minute felt eternal.

That depression aside, I am not alone in my problematical relationship with time. Think about some of the expressions that capture our struggles with the clock. First, those dealing with the weight of time: *Too much time on my hands. The Hours drag. The minutes seem like hours.* Then those expressions capturing the opposite experience when time seems too fleeting: *There are not enough hours in the day. I'm making up for lost time. Time is running out. Time is money. Race against time.* Our relationship with time can be vexing and subject to sudden shifts, not unlike our relationships with those we love.

I have a cousin who learned to avoid depression by keeping busy. My mother often mentioned this cousin, explaining that her problem disappeared once she realized that she got depressed when she had *too much time on her hands.* The expression itself bears contemplating. It is as if we are concretizing time, transforming a concept based on the apparent fundamental structure of the universe, a dimension in which events take place in sequence, into a material with physical properties we humans can take hold of and manipulate. When we say we have too much time on our hands, we are transforming time into a commodity, despite what we know about quantum mechanics and the Einsteinian universe. And just like money, we never seem to have the right amount.

In spite of what I've said about my adversarial relationship with time, hours, sometimes even days pass when I give little thought to their passing. Certainly, I'm generally aware of the progression of hours within each day as well as the momentum of the week through its seven days. And as we move toward the weekend, I can sense myself beginning to relax, opening more to pleasure, and feeling freedom from the constraints of the work week.

It would be more accurate to say, then, that my relationship with time is adversarial only when I think about it. And I ordinarily think about time only when there seems to be too much or too little. That is, until several days ago while I was sitting in my office meditating. Breathing in and out, letting thoughts enter my mind, then float away, I became aware of my clock ticking, and the longer I meditated, the more resonant the ticking grew. The slower and deeper I breathed — in and out, in and out — the fuller the ticks and tocks, each a drop of pond water teeming with life.

Suddenly, a mere minute, a division of time so insignificant that I have never really considered its capacity, appeared rich with possibility. Until then, minutes, like pennies, were to be squandered, not counted. *I'll be there in just a minute,* we might call out to our friend or partner, meaning we will be there in no time at all. *Just a minute,* an amount of time meant to sound so fleeting that it will hardly be noticed, too quick for the spark of impatience to ignite, too short to be deemed wasteful or impolite or tardy.

Sitting there meditating, watching my thoughts come and go, experiencing their transitoriness, understanding that nothing is permanent, I was supported by the steady and reliable ticking of the clock. And with this ticking, I became aware of just how large one minute is — or might be. I thought about all that could take place within the sixty seconds that accumulate to span a single minute. In one minute, a baby can be born. After hours of labor, of propulsion through and down the birth canal, after the crowning of the head and the tiny body slipping out into the wide world, the baby is not yet fully present in that world. But in less than a minute, the slippery, wet bundle who has just emerged sucks in his first breath of the air of this earth, and the fetus transforms into a baby, ushering in the true beginning of life.

In sixty seconds, an entire train can pass before your eyes. I know this. I have counted: fifteen cars, engine, boxcars, and passenger cars, and one caboose. In one minute, a sudden downpour can saturate the bone-dry fields of corn in central Illinois. In one minute, depending on the news, your life can change. In one minute, a person can pass over the border from living to dead.

My father is an astro-physicist. I told him about my new appreciation for a single moment in time and asked if he could supply any examples of rich time from outer space. Without hesitating, he asked if ten-to-the-minus-twenty-eighth of a second is small enough.

"Yes," I laughed. "So small that it's inconceivable."

"We now know everything that happened up to ten-to-the-minus-twenty-eighth of a second after the Big Bang," he said. "That's as close to t=0 as we can arrive."

Growing up, I had no aptitude for science. My best friend in college was also a physicist's daughter who understood nothing of her father's research; she and I created an entertaining routine, during which we imitated the various sounds our fathers' instruments made, mine in measuring cosmic ray intensity and hers registering imperfections in solids. I would begin: *beep, bebeep, bebeep, beep, beep.* And she would chime in: *scritch, scriiiiiiiitch, scriiiiiiiiiiiiiiitch, scritch.* Together, we were funny, and our friends never suspected how little we actually knew.

But my experience with the richness of a minute allowed me to follow my father's mini-lecture, so I was able to understand that, given what scientists now know about gravity and refraction, they can work their way back, creating a flow chart of all the chemical and physical changes that resulted from the explosion of the original fireball. But not quite all the way back. What actually took place in that ten-to-the-minus-twenty-eighth of a second we may never know. What we do know is that a great, great deal took place. Enough to set off life as we now know it and to make it possible for me to be sitting here thinking about time and how much can happen within so little of it. ▪

THE MOST IMPORTANT EVENT OF MY LIFE

Several months ago, a friend of mine participated in a workshop on creating ethical wills, and ever since has been struggling with writing one for herself. She finds the process of bequeathing her values and ethics to future generations daunting. Out of everything she believes and lives, how will she ever be able to select what to pass on to her daughters?

"I'm trying to pass down who I am to my family," she told me. "You know, my values, my hopes and fears, the most important events in my life. But there's so much to say, I don't know where to start."

"Did they give you any suggestions during the workshop?" I asked.

"They sent us home with a list of questions," she replied. "But I could write forever about each one."

"What's the first question?" I asked.

"What was the most important event in your life?"

"That's no help," I said. "No wonder you're having trouble. It would take me weeks just to decide what event to write about."

Ever since my friend and I had this conversation, I have been consumed with pinpointing a perfect response to a question I originally dismissed as ridiculous. Considering answers has become a near obsession. After all, if I'm a writer, I should be able to create a self-portrait and a plot for my life, and within this plot, zoom in on the turning point.

As a mother, I immediately gravitate toward Jonah's birth. After all, ever since he emerged from the birth canal, fists clenched, bright wide eyes scanning the delivery room, nothing has been the same for me . . . for any part of me. Ever since 2:17 A.M. on July 5, 1975, Jonah has floated in my consciousness, initially at dead center, now off to the edge, but always there. The velvet sound of his voice. The curls on his head. The curve of his little toes. He's with me perhaps on a more literal, physical level as well, for I recently read that male fetal cells circulate within the mother for the rest of her life, sometimes even raising havoc with her immune system. So Jonah's birth would be a suitable response to the ethical will question. Suitable, but much too large to write about in depth. And much too obvious for a writer, who is supposed to have an eye for the subtle.

The year I spent in India with my family was the next possibility to come floating up to me. Being seven at the time of our departure from Philadelphia to New Delhi and eight when we returned a year later, I was old enough to appreciate how exotic was everything I saw, ate, heard, and smelled, but not yet old enough to intellectualize my experience. As a result, I've carried around a well of images, tastes, sounds, smells, and sensations ever since, dipping into their waters often. I still crave Indian cuisine, am drawn to concerts of Bharatanatyam dance, and respond with every cell to Indian ragas. And I can sing the Indian National Anthem like a native New Dehlian.

But India is not really an event. It was a yearlong sojourn, itself composed of hundreds of heightened events. All these years later, it is still an endless slideshow on my mental screen. I remember my first day at the Muslim University Elementary School in Alighar, in the grassy courtyard, all my classmates circling round and pointing at me; the dance class, where I was handed my own set of tinkling ankle bells; dawn at the Ganges, hundreds of devotees wading in;

my first fiery taste of rogan josh; and the Taj Mahal by moonlight.

But although my year in India was precious and certainly formative, it was not a pivotal experience in my life. I did not decide to devote my college and graduate years to studying Indian dance or religions, did not return to live there, and did not become a world traveler. Instead, India became one of the eras in my life, a substratum upon which subsequent layers of my life experience formed themselves. If I dig down, I can recover much of that year, but the roots of the life I live now, my passions and my affinities, my joys and my miseries lie elsewhere.

And suddenly I know the answer. It strikes me like lightening, my heart and mind sizzling with the realization. The most pivotal event in my life? My assignment to an office at Lake Forest College when I first arrived there to teach French language and literature.

What could seem, on appearance, less consequential? Smaller? But its ordinariness and its complete lack of luster are what appeal to me. That, and the realization that the situation of my office at Lake Forest College did indeed lead to profound changes. Changes that altered the course my life had taken up to that point and eventually brought me to just where I am today.

With this insight, my life and the world along with it, both of which I usually experience as complicated, if not chaotic and full of contradiction and confusion, felt harmonious and ordered. Instead of the cacophony I often hear, melodic chords struck my ear. Rich chords, major chords. Ever since I was assigned that office at that small liberal arts college on Chicago's North Shore, all the events I can point to have played into the melody of my life.

I entered that office in the basement of Carnegie Hall, a collegiate Gothic building on the college's vast and graceful campus, as an instructor of French Language and Literature. Three years later, when I packed up my books and notebooks filled with notes for classes on Baudelaire and Flaubert and for teaching French verbs and leading conversations; when I emptied my desk drawers of pens and mechanical pencils, slips of paper with notes from students and colleagues, I was a student once again, off to study for an M.F.A. degree in poetry writing at the University of Iowa Writers' Workshop. I entered that office an academic, a specialist on the playwright Pierre Corneille, steeped in the world of dissertations and footnotes, theses and analyses, lectures and term papers. I left a poet, a young woman eager to turn her back on literary criticism and capture on the page what was symbolic and figurative, to create a personal universe where opposites could indeed transmute into something entirely unexpected.

It wasn't precisely the office itself that led to this transformation. It was its location next to the office of a young professor of writing. Hired to teach fiction and poetry writing, Mary Swander had just graduated from the Iowa Writers' Workshop. Fresh from Iowa City, she had a chapbook and a book-length manuscript on her resume, as well as honorable mention in the Yale Younger Poet's Series. Solid, full of the self-confidence bestowed by a degree from what was then the preeminent writing workshop, charged with her passion for poetry writing, she was everything I was not.

Despite my doctorate from the University of Michigan, I felt sorely underqualified for my position. Although I had once indeed been fluent in French, a language that had felt more my own than English, it had been some years since I'd been in France, and I was rusty. While I felt comfortable teaching a class that I had scripted, participating in French table every Wednesday night stirred up enough anxiety to render me mute. And I had never published! The one article I had written in haste when I was six months pregnant had been rejected from a prominent journal, and I lacked the courage or fortitude to submit it elsewhere.

Lake Forest prided itself on the amount of attention its faculty paid its students. Among other obligations, we were required to welcome students into our offices for appointments and drop-in visits at least three full days a week. I didn't mind this, for I enjoyed teaching and interacting with those in my classes. But at the time, foreign language study was at an ebb, all the language courses were underenrolled, and whole afternoons might pass with no visitors rapping on my door.

Mary Swander, however, was deluged. Day after day, students descended the stairs to her basement office, often lining up outside her door, waiting to discuss with her their latest story or group of poems. Always an eavesdropper, I couldn't help listening to the bits and pieces of conversation floating out into the hall. And I was immediately piqued. While I had been trained in graduate school to stand at an intellectual arm's length from the literature I taught, discussing the work's place in the literary cannon or isolating elements like symbolism and imagery or meter and form for analysis, Mary and her students entered into the heart of what they were discussing. Would the protagonist really behave like this? Did the climax of the story arrive too quickly? Was the symbolism organic to the content of the poem?

Imagine standing in a museum gallery and instead of positioning yourself several feet from a painting, you find yourself present at its creation, able to view the brush strokes as they are applied, the laying on of the various colors, the progressive accumulation of paint and line, so that the relationship of each tiny moment to the whole is revealed to you. How much more intensely you would engage with the canvas. How much more intimate your relationship with its meaning.

Several months into our first semester, I risked inviting Mary into conversation, timidly at first. I felt so ill-equipped to talk to her, so ignorant of the life and process of a writer. I had been educated as a literary critic, trained to cast my eye and intellect on works created by artists like Mary. I felt no more competent with her than I would have had a sculptor handed me a lump of clay and suggested that I work it. So I asked questions. How did she arrive at the metaphors in her poems? What criteria did she use for line breaks? Were all her decisions as far as word choice and rhyme conscious? Did she revise?

Slowly I became more fluent in the language of poetry writing. And more comfortable with Mary. At some point, she began showing me her poems, not only those she considered finished, but those in progress, those she was struggling to complete. I ventured comments. She took them seriously, sometimes even heeded my suggestions.

Looking back, the rest of my life seems to have unfolded from that office. I began to write, then entered the Iowa Writers' Workshop as a poet, and after several more twists and turns, including a stint at Stanford as an instructor in the Freshman English Program there, I became a writer and teacher of nonfiction.

Because of my office assignment, Mary and I became friends. And it is from my relationship with Mary Swander that my life was able to follow its ultimate course. If I had set up shop on the first or second floor of the Carnegie building instead of the basement, certainly I would have encountered Mary. But I would surely not have spent afternoons collecting snippets of conversation about the craft of fiction and poetry writing. And if I had not collected those snippets of conversation drifting into the hallway, I would never have approached Mary to engage her in a conversation about poetry. Without those conversations, I would certainly not have begun writing poetry. If I had not begun writing poetry, I would never have attended the Iowa Writers' Workshop. And without the Workshop, I would never have transformed myself from the academic I was trained to be to the writer I was meant to be; the writer who, with Mary, interviewed Midwestern gardeners and wrote *Parsnips in the Snow;* the writer who began teaching and coaching other writers; who wrote a second book, *Unstuck,* to help writers struggling with writing inhibitions; the writer I am today, practicing seeing small . . . and writing about it. ▪

PART TWO:

SCALING DOWN

Word by Word

A few months into seeing and thinking small, I discovered that each experience — spotting a dried leaf gracefully curled on the sidewalk or noticing the ripples of pleasure the smile of a stranger set off in me — remained alive for days, its memory launching one series of ripples after another. Not only could I recall the first moments of attention to the leaf or the smile, and once again experience what felt like the initial charge, but having re-experienced that original charge, I found myself musing about where and how the experience fit into my life and sense of self.

What did my joy at finding such beauty in a dead leaf tell me about the way I had lived up until that moment? How might this awareness of small change my life? And perhaps the essential question: Had I always been attracted to small but unaware of it until recently?

For years I preferred small spaces, small groups, and quiet moments that didn't overwhelm me with stimulation. Entering a roomful of people felt daunting, but I anticipated with pleasure meeting a friend for lunch or a walk. Shopping in a department store I experienced as chaotic, but I loved to browse in local boutiques. Wandering through an entire museum fatigued me, but I was often charged by a single exhibition.

Yet this current experience of small felt different. While in the past, large spaces, large groups, and entire museums made me retreat, shrink into myself, now I found myself expanding, beginning with a seed of small and enlarging upon that initial seed so that my experience intensified and became more vast. Instead of shrinking, I was growing.

And curiously, I was no longer either absent from or at the center of the experience. If I began by appreciating the grace of a dead leaf or the smile of a stranger, I was focused away from myself. Then slowly, as my appreciation grew, that grace or that warmth expanded to incorporate me within it. The process didn't start or end with me. It began with something in the world, outside of me, and concluded with my being a part of something much larger and more important than myself.

Once I realized the power of this new perspective, I decided to begin writing about it. Not about the perspective itself, but because they were so powerful, about each experience and its revelation. Without writing, which allows me to relive and reflect, I might be missing an important aspect or component of these flights into which small was launching me. I wanted to capture on the page the process that took me by the hand and led me from one hello to feeling embraced by the universe, or from preparing a single bowl of cranberry sauce to the communion of Thanksgiving dinner. I wanted, not to understand exactly what was happening to me, but to capture it in a way that it retained its power to set me free. A way that allowed me to reread what I had written and come close to that original experience.

Writing has always allowed me to make discoveries I might not otherwise make. I think this happens for several reasons. First, entering the flow of writing opens a part of my brain that remains inaccessible or much less accessible to me most of the time. It's that part of the brain we connect with when we meditate or practice yoga. A shy part of the brain that requires quiet and solitude to open up. It's a part of the brain easily overwhelmed by too much stimulation or noise. A part of the brain, I now realize, I feel quite kindred with.

Once I settle into my writing, a door opens and allows me access to feelings and ideas I'm unaware of. Capturing any of these ideas or emotions on the page leads me to yet other related ideas and emotions, which perhaps open new doors and windows, or simply lead me to even more ideas and emotions.

I may have originally seen the grace in a dried leaf curled on the sidewalk. And if I had continued contemplating the leaf without writing about it, I might well have been led to think of death and then to see a grace in death or dying I had never seen before. But writing about this same leaf after the initial experience, I found myself associating the leaf with dance and balletic movements of the human body.

From there, I visualized the dance of that particular leaf as it severed its relationship with the sycamore tree on the parking strip and floated downward to the sidewalk, catching perhaps a bit of breeze and uplift, then floating the rest of the way to its resting place, landing lightly on the sidewalk, and settling into its spot where the cement meets the grass, its right side curled toward the sky, its stem a soft C.

Having made this discovery through my writing, I realized that the leaf evoked both the sadness of life passing and the joy of a human body in motion, and that I am able to see these two very opposite emotions, not as a contradiction, but as parts of a whole and complex life experience. Writing about the leaf allowed me to discover all of this within a single moment: joy and sadness, stillness and motion, death and ballet.

Writing also presents the writer with another paradox. To write, you have to be focused on the present moment, on the page or computer screen, and on your hands moving across and down the page or tapping on your keyboard. But at the same time, writing frees you to travel in all dimensions, so that when writing, you may journey back into your past or forward into your future. I hadn't thought about the Cold War in years; it was an important part of my childhood, but had disappeared into the background of my life in the 1970s. Yet when I began writing about my neighbors' fierce quarreling, memories of life with my parents surfaced, and by association so did memories of the Cold War.

I realized something else as well, something that fills me with happiness: the act of writing means surrendering to small. For what else do we do when we write but focus on the here and now, the immediate? We pay attention to the page before us, the very sentence we are in the middle of, and the very word that we've just written. When we write, we put all else out of our minds but the person, the scene, the idea, the object we are writing about. We may begin with a broader, more muddled image, an amorphous, squiggly idea, a confused, swarming emotion. But once we set to the business of writing, once we are in the flow, the image concentrates, the idea clarifies, the emotion congeals. Through our writing we can zoom in upon, capture, and communicate the smallest moments of an experience, the tiniest segments of an image, the most minute aspects of a personality.

Of course, I didn't have to write about my experiences of small. They were rich and joy-inducing on their own. The writing wasn't necessary for me to return to each experience in the ensuing days, or to continue to reflect on that experience for some time. But I am a writer, and like a sunflower turning toward the sun, any intense experience turns me toward my writing.

Once I began writing, I didn't necessarily want to write about each of my experiences; I didn't want that sort of pressure. Rather, I wanted to be able to freely and clearly engage with some experiences, without their being yoked to an assignment to write. And writing about them all would have created a great deal of pressure, as well as demanded a tremendous amount of time. Once I realized how thinking and seeing small infused me with joy, the experiences began proliferating: not multiple times within a day, although that was sometimes true; and not even every day, but certainly several times each week.

I ended up writing about those experiences of small that resonated the most strongly and those that seemed the most important to me, those that led me on new byways or revealed additional powers of small. As I wrote about the most salient of these experiences, I gradually realized that small operated in my life in several ways. First, I could begin by noticing something within a larger canvas: a square inch within a crumbling wall, a single breath within the flow of breathing, one brushstroke in a painting. And as I remained present to the square inch, the breath, the stroke, what had begun as small would inflate into an experience — emotional or esthetic — of extreme pleasure, even joy.

I could also practice the opposite process. If I felt overwhelmed or depressed, enraged or pathetic, I could shrink my vision, scale down, so that instead of focusing on all that was wrong or too much in my life, I could rest my gaze on a small corner or moment or experience of pleasure or beauty within that chaos. And once I cleared my vision of the chaos and darkness, I was able, once again, to connect with the joy and pleasure in small.

Reflecting on all of this, I understood something more, something that helped me to grasp just why all these experiences seemed so profound and thrilling to me. I realized that each of my experiences of small was an entry point into the vast, glorious universe where I live. A conduit to my connection to something larger than myself, whether it be to Stephen and me as a couple whose love for each other continues to increase, or the possibilities for happiness and peace that surround me, or the community of humans I am part of. And all of this tells me, again and again, that I am never truly alone. ▪

ENDING THE COLD WAR

I WAS AMBLING ABOUT IN MY NEIGHBORHOOD, ADMIRING the last flush of floribunda roses, when furious, fierce screaming erupted from a house I was passing.

"You're just a piece of shit," a woman shrieked.

"You're a complete bitch," a man's voice snarled.

"Get out of here. I never want to see you again!" the woman screamed back.

Halfway down the block, I could still hear the commotion, although I was no longer able to make out the words. But it didn't matter. The warm air, which two minutes earlier had felt soft and embracing, was now polluted with the couple's animosity. I would carry the feeling for the rest of the day. That level of verbal violence made the world seem a brutal place, a minefield, where danger lurked behind the most aromatic rose or the tidiest hedge.

What had triggered such emotional brutality? How could two people who had set up a home together, who tended their flower beds, pruned their trees, arranged potted plants on their front porch reach that level of antagonism? What had gone wrong?

Then, as if a gale force wind was roaring over me, I recalled a recent argument I'd had with Stephen. He had forgotten, once again, to take out the garbage on trash day, and I was vexed. "I have to remind you every single week," I told him.

"So, I forget?" he replied. "It's not as if I refuse to help. "

"Why should I be the one who remembers? Why do I have to be the responsible person in this relationship?"

"I think you're exaggerating."

"You never remember to take out the trash!"

"Forgetting to take out the trash doesn't mean that I'm irresponsible. "

"I'm sick and tired of trying to remember everything for both of us!"

The argument continued, escalating, our voices rising, bodies rigid with rage.

"Don't you dare say I don't do anything around here."

"You don't. You take absolutely no responsibility for anything."

"So you're telling me I'm worthless. That I'm a piece of shit!"

Neither of us was about to concede. Quite the opposite. I grew more and more furious, while Stephen dug in his heels, determined to fend off my insults. He wouldn't apologize; he didn't think that not taking out the trash merited a heartfelt, "I'm sorry." And I continued to insist that my anger was justified. Once we had tired ourselves out, we simply let the matter drop, a cloud of resentment hovering above us for the rest of the evening.

Stephen and I never resolve our arguments. Either the issue becomes a fierce tug of war, each of us straining and pulling until exhaustion sets in, or I escalate until he backs down. Not because we have reached an understanding or even a compromise, but because I have raised the ante dangerously high: "I'll be fine without you!" And though, of course, I don't really mean what I say, Stephen feels trounced.

An hour or two afterward, or at the very latest, the next day, I begin to soften. *Oh,* I think, *how could I have gotten so angry over the trash? What is wrong with me?* My heart quickens as

I remember how much I love Stephen. Suddenly, whatever we had been arguing about — the trash, his messy office, even money — seems insignificant next to the swell of tenderness I now feel for him. *How could I have become so incensed? So enraged at somebody I love?*

For my parents, no disagreement was ever small. One tiny spark and their entire relationship went up in flames. My father was the arsonist, my mother the self-declared victim of his match. One peccadillo and instantly their language flared hyperbolic. *Always. Uncaring. Cruel.* As a consequence, I am unschooled in the diplomacy of give and take, of back and forth, of slowly filling the gap in perspective or opinion between two people. I never witnessed my parents shortening the distance between them, even one tiny step; never saw their arms outstretched toward that other person they had lived with for twenty, thirty, forty, fifty years, with whom they conceived and raised two children, next to whom they had slept for an incalculable number of nights.

Judging from their all-encompassing rage, neither had the couple I heard screaming ugliness at one another that afternoon. They seemed to be fighting to the death, as if difference is necessarily fatal and unhappiness with a partner's behavior inevitably terminal, as if every disagreement between two people demands not simply fight or flight, but both responses simultaneously.

Looking back at my childhood and the dynamic between my parents, I am reminded of the Cold War, with the progressive escalation of the competition between the United States and the Soviet Union. As tensions between the powers increased, the economic pressure, diplomatic maneuvering, propaganda, assassinations continued to rise. Along with the stakes, the rhetoric escalated: *Pinko, Commie, Godless, Evil Empire . . .*

I remember so well the air raids at my elementary school, all the children lining up to leave their classrooms and crouch along the walls in the long, dark corridors with their gleaming linoleum floors, heads lowered into our hands. I remember talk of bomb shelters in backyards. Of radiation poisoning. Of the end of the world.

We never knew when the alarm would sound: we could be settled into our reading groups, sounding out words from *Fun With Dick and Jane,* or sitting at our desks practicing cursive, when a long blast from the air raid siren would send us scurrying to form two lines near the classroom door, then tiptoe out into the hall.

It wasn't all that different at home. A wrong word or response from my mother could enrage my father and lead to an explosion as we sat around the maple table for dinner. Or in the car, my brother and I in the backseat, en route to visit my paternal grandparents in Manhattan, my mother might chide my father for not standing up to his mother the last time we visited, and the car would suddenly swerve into the far-right lane, my father screaming that he was going to turn around and take my mother back home.

In the end, the Cold War remained just that — cold. It never heated up enough for concrete hostilities to erupt. Rather, tensions seethed below the surface, their prickles becoming a way of life for all of us, decade after decade, through the Fifties, the Sixties, the Seventies, and well into the Eighties.

Perhaps the Cold War is more than a historical metaphor for the relationship between my parents, between the couple in my neighborhood, between Stephen and me. Maybe what I meant as figurative applies in a literal way as well. The vicious fights and arguments many couples engage in might be the manifestations of the state in which they live, much of the time apparently calm on the surface, with resentments and anger steeping just below. Perhaps that is why small disturbances escalate so easily . . . why I can leap from one incident of not taking out the trash to Stephen's global irresponsibility . . . why, when a close friend of mine tripped on an object her husband had failed to put away, the emotional spark jumped from that one object to her husband's generalized laziness and incompetence . . . why the couple whose house I passed the other afternoon so quickly escalated from anger to banishment.

Today, the violence of the neighbor's fight still stalking me, I ask myself: *What if I dispose of the rope I haul out for our tugs of war? What if I lower the ante of my quarrels with Stephen? If instead of escalating, we try diminishing the scope of our disagreement? Instead of letting the spark catch, then fanning the flames with our anger, we resist lighting the match in the first place? What if we leave the debris in place, the pile of leaves, the untended trash, the unpaid bill, the forgotten meeting, the overlooked request, and work together to solve this one particular problem we are currently facing? What if, instead of broadening our perspective, we narrow it? What if we put emotional blinders on?*

The first time I thought seriously about the blinders placed over horses' eyes, the practice upset me. How terrible it would be to limit any creature's vision, I thought. But reading more about the situations in which blinders are used, I understood their value. Blinders curtail a horse's view only when what he sees out of the corners of his eyes might distract or frighten him, causing him to spook, imperiling both the horse and the rider.

Emotional blinders, in certain situations, might do the same for couples. They might block out all the other perceived infractions our partner may have committed in the past and might commit in the future. After all, the past is behind us, and the future is unknown. It is the present we are engaged with, and it is in the present that the problem has presented itself. Blinders might prevent the debris of the past from intruding on the present and impinging on the future of a relationship.

Of course, relationships transcend the present. My love for Stephen has a definite past, a history. I can remember the moment I knew I could love him. I had met him several days earlier, then

I ran into him one afternoon while I was dropping Jonah off at the orthodontist's. As I was maneuvering into a parking place on a narrow Berkeley street, Stephen happened to drive by. He pulled up beside my car, lowered his driver's window, and leaned back into the seat. It was late in the afternoon, the sun beginning to sink, and it cast its light onto his face through the window, illuminating his smile. He looked so kind and relaxed, so expansive, as if he had all the time — and intention — in the world to sit there in his car on the narrow Berkeley street and talk to me.

Thinking back to that afternoon, I hope that from now on, when confronting a problem in the present, Stephen and I both stop before we react, taking a moment to remind ourselves who our "opponent" is and the deep feelings we have toward him or her. Then, infused with our love or admiration or passion or tenderness, we can isolate the current offense and together discuss strategies for solving that one problem. If it turns out that Stephen indeed never remembers, not ever, to take out the trash, we might renegotiate our division of labor. Or he might invent a mnemonic to remind him that Thursdays are trash days. Or I might decide that, even though Stephen never remembers the trash, reacting intensely and arguing fiercely are never productive responses. Being angry isn't worth it. Escalation leads to nuclear fallout. I might even realize that simply considering resisting the impulse has brought me back to that afternoon twenty years ago when I first felt the grace of Stephen's smile. ▪

JUST HELLO

THE OTHER NIGHT, PREPARING DINNER WITH JONAH'S friend Naomi, a newly-minted nurse practitioner, I realized that as she told me about her new job, she was offering me yet another lesson in small.

Naomi is a young woman with fierce ideals and the passion to realize them. After graduating with a B.A. in English, she went back to school to become an R.N., then studied for her nurse practitioner's degree, putting in a large chunk of time and money, so she could offer medical help to the homeless in San Francisco. As soon as she graduated, she began working for two different agencies, one a community health center serving a predominantly Latino population, the other an organization ministering to a group of once homeless people now living in single occupancy rooms in The Tenderloin.

When she began this work, Naomi expected to do a great deal of medical healing. She even hoped to save lives. After all, many of her clients had been living on the streets for quite a while without roofs over their heads, to say nothing of medical care. As a nurse practitioner, she was licensed not only to diagnose, but to intervene. She could order lab tests, prescribe medication, even order hospitalization. And indeed, she has been able to do some of this. She recognized one client's discomfort as a heart attack. She diagnosed another's bleeding as a cancer symptom. And she has prescribed medication for countless cases of pneumonia, a common illness among the homeless, who often have little shelter from the raw, damp San Francisco weather.

But she quickly discovered that the majority of her cases involve medical routine: bandaging wounds, ordering blood tests, and prescribing antibiotics; saving lives happened less frequently. And she was disappointed. More distressing were the clients she wasn't able to help medically. After all, she was trained in medicine, and it was through the application of what she had learned that she expected her clients to benefit. Yet a great many of them didn't seem to want medical intervention, and some people outright refused it. They might come to her to complain of this or that, some of it potentially grave, but when she suggested a medical remedy, they shook their heads, no thanks. One man stumbled into her cubicle of an office grasping his chest and complaining of pain. Naomi sat him down and dialed 911. But when the medics arrived, the client refused to go to the hospital. "No," he insisted, "I got better things to do."

"But you are most likely having a heart attack," Naomi said. "And it could be fatal. You could die," she insisted, hoping that the mention of "death" might convince him of the urgency of his condition.

But he continued shaking his head. "I told you, I got better things to do."

Over and over again, Naomi experienced similar reactions. And each time, she felt as if she had failed. Not only was she not able to heal some of her client population, she was not able to convince them to allow others more knowledgeable than herself to intervene. Again and again, her clients had better things to do, were too wary of doctors and hospitals to surrender to their care, or too racked on drugs to understand the gravity of their medical situation.

Then one day, about a month after his chest-pain incident, the man who had "better things to do" stopped by Naomi's cubicle. "Hello," she said, when she saw him standing in the doorway. "What seems to be the trouble today?"

"Nothing," he answered. "Just stopped by to say hello."

Not long after this, a woman in the last stages of lung cancer dragged herself in to Naomi's office to ask if Naomi would stop in her room to visit her once in a while. "That would feel real good," the women told Naomi. The woman was in the care of a physician and could still attend to her own needs, so Naomi understood that her request had little to do with Naomi's official capacity at the site. What the woman was requesting was something quite different than medical care; she was asking Naomi for a moment of attention. A moment of contact every few days to create a bridge between living and dying, between herself, a woman who had lived on the street most of her life, with no friends and family, and whose lungs had been invaded by cancerous cells that were now choking her, and radiant Naomi, beloved by her family and friends, bursting with health and hope and healing.

Naomi slowly began to understand her role in a new way, a less obviously heroic and interventionist way. A smaller way. While some of what she provided was medical intervention, at times lifesaving, her usefulness extended far beyond prescriptions, calls to 911, and diagnoses. She was there to offer her simple presence to her clients, to extend a hand, a hello, a nod of the head in their direction. She was there to provide the slightest contact, a moment of connection to these clients who had been alone and abandoned for so much of their life.

"And so I realized," she told me, "that some of the smallest things I could do were crucially important to the people I work with and for." Just saying hello, for instance, might be the first moment in a relationship that could grow enough to allow Naomi entrée when crucial medical intervention was needed.

As Naomi reflected, I thought of an interview I had seen with the Uruguayan writer Eduardo Galeano, a charming man, who could talk comfortably about just about everything, from politics to relationships, without sounding high-minded or arrogant. When asked what he wrote about, Eduardo replied, "I write about the greatness of small things. Many people think that large is great," he continued, "but they are wrong. I am absolutely sure that greatness lies only in what is small."

What Galeano meant by small, as he made clear a bit later, is the ordinary man and the ordinary events in which he becomes involved. Not heroes and heroics, not revolutions or earth-shattering discoveries, but events like farm laborers plowing the fields or harvesting the crops, year after year, day by day, the essential link in bringing food to our tables so we can eat. By "small" he meant, surely, the workers in their jumpsuits and hardhats repairing our highways or building or skyscrapers, men whose lives, overlooked by so many of us, ensure that our commerce forges ahead, that the crops move from one coast to the other, that we all have milk and eggs and cheese in our refrigerators. Small men and small lives, upon whose shoulders the wellbeing of a country resides. Small men, whose actions are viewed as anything but heroic by most of the people they serve.

When I was in my twenties and thirties, I used to pour over the "People" section of *Time*, admiring the achievements of the men and women featured on its pages. These were not the Hollywood celebrities of today's fame, but men and women, some young, some middle-aged, who had done something important and prominent with their lives. And they were being rewarded for it. I suffered by comparison, a Ph.D. with a mediocre job, exiled in a small town in the Midwest. My then-husband, Barry, liked to joke with our friends, "Jane's the only person I know who compares herself to the "People" section in *Time!*"

As Naomi and I talked in my kitchen, I thought of my younger self: the self who thought I should be doing something more, something larger; the self who was certain it was not enough just to publish an article from my dissertation if it didn't appear in the foremost academic journal; the self who thought it didn't count to be teaching at a small Midwestern liberal arts college when everyone knew only Princeton, Brown, or Columbia mattered; the self who considered staying home with my newborn son embarrassing. I should have been juggling teaching, nursing my baby, preparing elegant meals, and volunteering at the local soup kitchen.

I haven't yet outgrown this self who tends to discount my professional life because it is insignificant: *I'm just . . . , it's just . . . , it doesn't really count.* I find myself apologizing because my garden isn't glorious. I chide myself because I am doing nothing for the world, where people suffer and die, while instead I sit at my computer and write pieces that are far from spectacular.

But listening to Naomi, I found myself thinking: *Now, perhaps, I am ready to move beyond my self-deprecation.* Thanks to Naomi, who is devoting herself to the homeless, who has learned how far a simple hello can travel, and has brought back to me the words of a great writer. Together, Naomi and Galeano remind me of the importance of small acts and ordinary people. ▪

Small Favors

When a woman who lived around the block from me died suddenly several weeks ago, a neighbor adopted the woman's eleven-year-old cat. To make certain the bonding went well, she left the cat in her familiar home, visiting her twice a day, until she considered the cat ready for the move.

Last week I noticed a sign on our community bulletin board: "Traumatized cat needs good home." The next time I ran into the adopting neighbor, I mentioned the announcement. "It was awful," she exclaimed. "The cat clawed a hole in our guest room mattress and spent her days curled inside. At night she emerged and mewled for hours on end."

"That doesn't sound viable," I commiserated.

"After a few days, I was so sleep deprived I couldn't function. But I'm such a rescuer, it was hard for me to give her up."

I have friends who are rescuers. When one friend hears of somebody ailing, she makes a pot of chicken soup, which she delivers to their door. I know a man who's been married three times, and in each marriage, he played the role of the knight in shining armor, rescuing one wife from severe depression, another from an abusive husband, and the third from a disabling illness.

I'm always impressed by the acts of courage and heroism I read about in the newspapers. During the Katrina catastrophe, articles featured doctors leaving their private practices to spend weeks in New Orleans tending the sick. Several animal lovers I know joined the efforts to rescue family pets stranded in the Louisiana floods. Others immediately adopted storm-orphaned dogs or cats.

When I hear about people reaching out or sacrificing in any measure to help others in need, I wonder about my own inertia when it comes to charity. I have friends who work at soup kitchens; several people I know volunteer with Hospice; two women friends spend one afternoon a week cuddling crack babies at the hospital; another friend heads the local Christmas in April, an organization that revitalizes and restores the homes of low-income elderly and disabled. Somebody else I know spends a month each year in rural China ministering to the sick. And a friend of my son made several trips to Uzbekistan volunteering her services toward whatever needed to be done.

My volunteer history is thin. When I was a freshman in college, I joined a Big Sister program for girls living in the Rhode Island Children's Shelter. I have only dim memories of this experience, mainly centered on the long bus ride and the bleak setting, where we roamed about with our charges for an hour each Friday afternoon until we once again boarded the bus and returned to our dormitories on the Hill. I joined this program at the urging of a friend, who came from a civic-minded family, and my main reaction to the experience was of the futility of our efforts.

It's difficult to admit that my next stint at charity work took place over twenty years later when I volunteered one Thanksgiving to serve the holiday meal at Glide Memorial Church in San Francisco. And although my effort might be viewed as philanthropic, this time my motive was actually selfish. After twenty-one years together, my husband and I had just separated, and I couldn't decide where or how to celebrate Thanksgiving. My friends were all generous; I could have spent the day with any number of families. But finding myself for the first time without a family of my own, I felt awkward inserting myself into the traditions of somebody else's table and thought it would be wiser to find a neutral site to celebrate the day. Glide Memorial Church, well known for its soup kitchen, and even better for its Thanksgiving and Christmas meals, seemed a perfect alternative.

I felt pleased with my decision. In addition to providing me the perfect alibi for friends and family, I looked forward to spending the day surrounded by volunteers who were generously spending part of their own holiday creating one for the needy. But when I arrived at the church, I discovered that too many volunteers had appeared on the scene, and we were to work in shifts. The arrangement left me cooling my heels outside the church for over an hour until my shift was summoned; then I was allowed to serve for only an hour, which meant I was back on BART on my way home by 2:00 P.M. on Thanksgiving afternoon.

I might have viewed the overabundance of volunteers as a good thing. Wasn't it inspiring that so many people were willing to serve the poor? But inside the Church, the *esprit de corps* was anything but inspiring. Once my group received its marching orders, the crew worked the entire hour in silence, scooping potatoes, slicing turkey, ladling soup, all without exchanging a word. Neither the volunteers nor the diners conversed: no greetings, no pleasantries, not even any smiles.

Charity is meant to flow away from the provider and toward the recipient. And because gratitude should not figure into the equation, I do not mention my wan experiences as the cause of my passivity when it comes to public acts of kindness. If I'm thinking about the Rhode Island Children's Shelter and Glide Memorial Church now, it is because I'm trying to fathom just why I have never been prone to such acts. And as a cognate of that question, I'm wondering just how large, how heroic the act needs to be to count.

JANE ANNE STAW

I understand that behavior toward others can never be seen in a vacuum. Certainly, we view some acts as universally heroic, regardless of context. Michael Keenan, a Berkeley man who rushed into his friend's burning house to save the friend's beloved dog, died recently as a result of his burns. Several years earlier, he had rescued a woman when her car dived into the San Francisco Bay. Without a doubt, this man is heroic.

One of my neighbors volunteered to donate a kidney to the San Francisco Live Organ Program. Although she will not be putting her health seriously at risk, she will certainly incur discomfort and inconvenience in the process of saving somebody else's life. In my eyes, any action that saves another's life, no matter what the circumstances, is heroic.

More frequently, however, it is the situation of the giver that determines just how generous her actions might be. If my chicken-soup-delivering friend worked sixty hours a week in a corporate law firm, her pot of chicken soup might be considered heroic. How in the world did she find time to stop at the store, clean, then simmer the bird for hours, skim the foam, cool and strain the liquid, then deliver the nourishing broth to her friend or acquaintance? However, if she doesn't hold a demanding job and often finds herself with time on her hands, the act, although certainly kind, might no longer be viewed as a sacrifice.

Of course, great acts of charity don't necessarily involve great personal risk or sacrifice. In fact, we have a term, unsung hero, to describe those who regularly commit such acts without drawing attention to their behavior. In these cases, it is often the persistence of a person's generosity, not the magnitude of what they offer that makes them worthy of the title. A volunteer fireman who has served for years and years without reward quickly comes to mind. Or the crossing guard who stands sentinel at the busy intersection of a local elementary school each morning for a quarter century. The absence of fanfare and recognition also create unsung heroes. Here, my neighbor would qualify, for I am one of the few people she has told of her intention to donate a kidney. Giving up something for another — either time, money, or physical wellbeing — without seeking or earning praise is my definition of heroic.

Books have been written about generosity, many proposing its biological basis. Evolutionary theorists explain altruism as a form of kin inclusion: we are generous to those to whom we are related. Others point to gene-based mechanisms to explain our kindness to others. Whatever the precise cause, it might well be that generosity is hardwired in us. But I wonder if physiology and biology can explain all acts of kindness. There is something to be said here for nurture. The family that raises us can either instill in us a belief in charity or nourish that impulse, if indeed it exists within our soul from the very outset.

While charity was not a value inculcated in my family, apart from the annual donations to the Allied Jewish Appeal and the United Fund, many of the people I know who spend time working for others were raised in families where service was an important value. But not all. Last night at dinner, a friend spoke about her son, who is visiting Mali, where he volunteered for the Peace Corps. During his Peace Corps stint, he became close with a young man named Nigeria, who ran the local store in the small town where my friend's son was working. When he returned to Mali for a visit after several years, my friend's son worried about Nigeria, who appeared quite jaundiced and weak. He and his girlfriend, who traveled with him on the trip, decided to take Nigeria to the hospital, which is located in Bamako, thirteen hours away by bus.

My friend told this story not to brag but to marvel over the generosity of her son. She was pleasantly surprised by his action. Spending several days of a vacation taking a friend to a hospital is her son's very personal response to his friend's illness.

My friend's son's generosity is more focused than the generosity of the people I know who volunteer to tutor or work in soup kitchens. His act will not serve the public good, but the good of one very particular individual. Hearing this story, I couldn't help but wonder what I would have done in a similar situation. Am I capable of such a large gesture, a commitment of a substantial amount of time and energy on behalf of a friend? And given that my friend's son's act is so very circumscribed, is it smaller than acts that promote a larger good?

While I was trying to sort out these questions, one of my clients unwittingly provided a response. When she came for her appointment yesterday, several days before I was due to travel to New York, she was feeling queasy. "If I'm ill, I don't want to pass this on to you, but I don't think it's anything," she assured me. "My husband made me a smoothie this morning, chock full of supplements, and I think it didn't agree with me." I told her I wasn't concerned, and we proceeded with our appointment.

Today, she left me a message. "I just wanted to reassure you in case you were worried. By late in the afternoon I felt fine. You don't have to worry about catching anything from me!"

This client is a rescuer. Family, friends, children — she ignores her own wellbeing to save them unhappiness or inconvenience. She is capable of the grandest of actions and the greatest of self-sacrifices. Yet listening to her message, which involved no sacrifice on her part, I felt uplifted. Here was somebody who cared, who didn't want me to worry. Her concern penetrated me like a balm, layer by layer, cell by cell, infusing me with its warmth. As I hung up the phone, I understood that even the smallest acts can save those of us who didn't even know we needed to be rescued. ▪

Scaling Down

I HAVE ALWAYS REACTED INTENSELY TO MY ENVIRONMENT. Derelict buildings, untended gardens, living rooms full of disorganized clutter make me queasy. My stomach churns, I feel dizzy and unfocused, my breathing turns shallow. Stephen, a visual artist accustomed to defining images in terms of color, tone, scale, and hue, used to find my response incomprehensible.

"I feel it in my body," I'd tell him.

"In your body?" he would laugh.

"Yes," I insisted, "in my body."

The deep structure of my malaise varies with the situation. Walk me into a living room with magazines and books strewn about, newspapers cluttering the floor, dirty cups and saucers abandoned next to chairs and sofa, used plates piled, and I am overcome by a feeling of chaos. No matter what my state of mind just minutes earlier, the laws of gravity no longer seem to hold; while I tumble over and over, unable to keep my feet anchored on the floor, the earth spins, launching me toward a black hole. Standing before a derelict building — its windows shattered, walls covered in layers of graffiti, façade crumbling — no matter where I am physically, I feel I am standing in a vast urban desert, the lone survivor of a cataclysm. Put me in front of a neglected garden and I am utterly alone, abandoned by even those I believed were my closest family and friends.

In my own home and garden, I am able to work with this hair-trigger reactivity. Stephen has come to respect my need for order and aesthetic harmony. Since he is a collector by nature, and I a discarder, this took a bit of time and negotiating. During his most intense period of buying African masks and Kuba cloth, he agreed to be very selective about what we displayed, while I consented to regular "exhibit" shifts. And although he finds a dining room table with the day's newspaper splayed out a homey sight, he now refolds the paper each morning once he's finished reading.

This physical response to my environment isn't all negative. Beauty and order uplift me. A tidy living room, where the furniture and accessories are balanced and complementary, a garden of thriving and harmonized plants, a building that has been recently restored with a smart paint job and new landscaping, all put me into a state of relaxation. My breathing deepens and slows, the muscles in my face relax, and I feel as if every cell in my body is gently floating and circulating.

For many years, I had no way to quell my intense response to unfortunate aesthetics in the world I wandered through each day. But a recent shift in my vision has changed all that. One day, after I parked my car and was walking toward Stephen's studio, a downspout, rusted into an intricate pattern of swirls, caught my eye. I happened to have my camera slung over my shoulder, so I stopped to take a photo from across the street in order to capture the downspout from top to bottom. But when I checked the shot in my viewfinder, I realized that what surrounded the downspout — peeling doors and broken windows — cluttered the shot and obscured what had originally attracted me. So I moved closer and took another picture, this time zooming in on a portion of the downspout. This shot was better, with fewer detracting elements, but it still didn't capture my original vision. Looking carefully at the second shot in the viewing screen, I realized that my eye, amid all the deterioration and debris, had been able to home in on and isolate a very small part of the whole to admire. How to help my camera do the same? So I moved much closer to the rust, and at a distance of not more than a foot, shot pictures from above and below, left and right. When I reviewed these shots, what I saw astonished me. No longer was I looking at a rusted-out downspout, but at a series of abstract paintings filled with iridescent blues and oranges and blacks.

Marveling at these images, I realized that there are alternate ways of viewing the world. Certainly at times, I need to consider the whole, the large or full picture. Without this long view, my world would shrink dramatically, and I would no longer know where I was, either geographically or intellectually. But the long view isn't the only view. I also have the option of focusing on a portion of the whole. And the size of this portion depends on what I hope to understand or perceive.

To avoid the discomfort I used to experience so intensely, I learned that I could see smaller. Instead of taking in the entire abandoned building I am passing — the crumbling stucco; the rusted and dented pipes; the filthy, jagged windows — I could focus on much less. I could isolate a moment in the façade, a single pipe, or one window, and perhaps something completely new would appear to me.

And that is exactly what continued to happen. When I next fixed my gaze on a few square inches of the exterior stucco of that same building, what I saw thrilled me. No longer dirt and grime and decay, the building façade became a mosaic of hieroglyphics and shades of gray: dove, silver, slate, charcoal, and mist. Other rusted areas flamed filigrees of rust so delicate they took my breath away.

Since that moment, I've seen so much beauty. A filthy window now becomes a canvas on which the sun paints its iridescence, a dying vine draped over a chain-link fence is a delicate ribbon. Cracks in concrete appear as sinuous rivers, dried coffee at the bottom of a cup is a burnt sun. My initial response to decay hasn't changed. But now, my malaise becomes a reminder to shift my perspective to small and discover what beauty the scene before me has to offer.

Lately, I've taken to wandering about old industrial or abandoned areas with my camera. Whenever I come upon a particularly decrepit or ruined building, I first take a photo of the whole, from a distance. Then I begin moving closer and closer, isolating with my lens smaller and smaller moments to allow the beauty they contain to emerge. Printing these series of shots taken in succession is revelatory; they take the viewer, looking at the same building, step by step, from blight to beauty.

The world has become so much more inviting for me. My new experience has taught me that there is beauty everywhere, often where we least expect it. I can move from a sunset by the Pacific Ocean, with its fiery layers of red and orange, to garbage washed up on the beach, where I spot a rusted bottle cap that has morphed into a delicate disk, and each experience captivates me in a different way. The sunset will expand me, pulling my gaze from the ocean in front of me to the horizon and then on to thoughts of other people and other shores on the far side of the vastness.

The bottle cap, with its intricate etching of water and time, leads me inward. Like a spider launching a nearly invisible filament, it connects me with myself and my joy at discovering overlooked or discarded moments. *I find this beautiful*, I think. Exquisite as well. And at that moment, I love not only the world more, but myself as well. ▪

Near at Hand

I'M STRUGGLING WITH MY FAMILY ONCE AGAIN. NOT WITH Jonah or Stephen, but with my parents and my brother. The struggle is nothing new. My fifty-six-year-old brother is a drug addict, and each time he leaves a treatment program or disappears for several days, everybody's antennae quiver. We're all on edge, tense, trying not to expect bad news. But quivering antennae is not really the problem. My mother is. She cannot follow the protocol we've established for dealing with my brother's lapses, and when she's worried about him, she lashes out at me. This too is nothing new. It's been happening for a lifetime. But though I'm aware of the pattern, even expect and predict it, I feel wounded. And angry. And sorry for myself. All in the largest possible way. It's as if I'm a pond my mother has tossed a stone into, and as the ripples of the splash widen, everything in my life becomes unstill and wavery.

The first ripples find me hurt about the current interaction. I feel unfairly treated, unappreciated. After all the energy I've spent on my brother, all the hours I've sat and talked with him, all the appointments I've chauffeured him to, how could my mother find fault with me? My behavior has been exemplary. I've remained calm and compassionate, negotiating fraught interactions among my mother, father, brother, and me. Not once did I speak out when something my mother said or did went against the advice of our drug counselor, undermining the plan of action we had all agreed upon. Not once did I mention that I suspected my brother of lying. And I certainly never said a word about how painful it was to sit across from him at a restaurant and watch his eyes rolling back into his head.

Those are only the first, the tiniest, ripples. The next find me sobbing internally because my mother has never loved me, has always preferred my brother. While I was the good and dutiful daughter who brought home pristine report cards, walked and fed the family dog, and ran errands for her over the weekend, my brother was transferring from school to school, plucking money from my father's wallet, and shaking a threatening fist at my mother whenever she refused his requests for money. Each time, my mother absolved him, invoking his inherent sweetness, while in my case, an innocent shrug or an inadvertent frown were evidence of my disrespect and meanness.

Quickly, I escalate from feeling my mother doesn't love me to feeling universally unloved. And unlovable. I am deluged by proof. In the seventh grade, my best friend conspired against me with another girl, snickering about me at our lockers, squeezing me out of our social set and the weekend parties. And in high school, the senior class president I was dating dropped me for one of my best friends. I heard the news in the cafeteria, over macaroni and cheese, and was forced to scurry into the girls' room to hide my tears. Quickly, my life of rejection is swirling around me, slights and misunderstandings circling me like a school of fish.

Once the ripples have spread this far, the circumference of the circle is quick to include my being a globally bad person, someone riddled with flaws, someone who deserves her mother's anger, who doesn't deserve her mother's love.

By this time, I'm ripping out all the stitches of my life, undoing everything I've ever accomplished, focusing on all that has gone wrong: my first marriage, several friendships, my relationship with my mother; and what I've never accomplished: publishing my dissertation as a book, having more than one child, selling enough copies of my book *Unstuck*.

My only solace is that I know I'm not alone. Just this morning, I received a message from a student who condemns herself because she is forty-two and still single. "My whole life is a failure," she wrote, forgetting about her successful career as a grant writer and the fact that she is currently a student in a demanding M.F.A. program in writing. And if I knew her better, I'm certain I could list plenty of other successes she turns her back on when she pillories herself.

Several months ago, a friend, who has a contract for a book with a major publisher, planned a trip to Costa Rica. At first, she was happy to travel alone, anticipating encountering people along the way. Then she met a woman who asked to travel with her, and my friend was thrilled. When the newfound friend became ill and could no longer leave the country, my friend fell into despair, not only over traveling to Costa Rica alone, but also about the book she was writing. In her mind, her vacation was ruined. Her book was trivial and writing is a great struggle; she was stupid to think she could write a book. Everything goes wrong in her life.

Why is it that so often, when something goes awry, so many of us quickly escalate and generalize, creating a bridge between whatever small thing has gone poorly to everything else in our lives that feels unresolved and less than stellar? Why is the pull toward negativity so strong? And why can't our successes breed as quickly? Where have we learned to be so hard on ourselves? What mathematician devised the formula for computing failures and mistakes?

I've read that while many women feel responsible for their mistakes and losses and tack their successes up to chance, more men react in the opposite way, taking responsibility for gains and blaming failures on bad luck . . . or on others. From my experience, this research finding is valid. Something goes wrong, and my women friends think of all the ways the failure is their fault; while quite a few of the men I know look around and rope in somebody else to blame.

Of course, at their core, both responses are the same: reactions to disappointment. Not only that, they share the ripple dynamic; both men and women expanding outward from the glitch itself. But while women remain at the epicenter of their expansion, men try desperately to relocate that center elsewhere.

What's clear is that, no matter our gender, disappointment and trouble send many of us off on lengthy travels as we spin our unhappiness further and further from the initial sting. What if, instead, we remained closer to home? And I mean this quite literally. What if we stopped ourselves from spiraling outward and looked around us to see what catches our attention and allows us to find solace in pleasures we can discover near at hand?

My house is filled with Stephen's paintings. And although I have admired each one, either while he was creating it or when we first framed and hung it on our walls, it's been quite some time since I've allowed any of them to captivate me once again. So much else seems to demand my attention, especially the routines of daily life. Yet today, when I am brooding over family tension, I find myself gazing at a painting of a woman whose downcast aqua eyes seem to share my sorrow. Unlike me, however, she appears relaxed, her forehead luminous, her supple mouth ripe with silence, her neck long and graceful. As I watch her, I wonder if her eyes are not cast downward, as I first thought, but inward, away from the source of her pain and sorrow, toward the soul that will sustain her.

Gazing at the painting, I see not only the woman, but the hand of my husband, who created her. I see this in the colors he has chosen, pale mauve for her hair, a light mint for the background, and fleshy orange, chrome yellow, and rose for subtle accents. I see him as well in the brushstrokes and shading, light illuminating the center of her face, rendering the bridge of her nose nearly invisible, while color rises delicately on her cheeks. In the intricate mosaic he creates within selected cracks, I see him poised before his easel in his studio, dipping the slender brush he pinches between his thumb and forefinger into tiny bottles of acrylic, then dabbing the tip onto the surface, wiping away excess with the fleshy heel of his hand or tip of his index finger.

Gazing at this woman, I understand that I am able to embrace and feel embraced by this painting, not necessarily because it was created by Stephen, but because looking closely at any work of art reveals the hand of the artist. In the bold brushstrokes of a Diebenkorn landscape, I can feel the movement of the artist's hand and arm sweeping across the canvas, dipping here and rising there. Focusing on a Georgia O'Keeffe flower, I can sense her gaze reaching beyond the petals to the pistils and stamen. And if I allow my attention to cling to the image, I can feel my gaze merging with hers, as if I am entering the flower along with O'Keeffe, diving deep into its throat, becoming intoxicated by the mingling of its textures and aromas, a velvety sweetness embracing me.

Today, I rise from the chair where I am sitting and step closer to Stephen's painting, peering until my nose nearly grazes the image. Now it is the surface that pulls me in, its tiny pits and shadings, moments when mauve and mint green meet and overlap, merging into something new that echoes each of its components: a tiny child carrying within traces of father and mother and, at the same time, rich with possibility. Each moment of the painting is like a cell embodying the entire painting: its colors, brushstrokes, shadings, lines, image . . . and more, the hands of the artist, his callused knuckles, splayed tips of fingers, full-mooned nails. And even more, for the hands of the artist, my husband, are extensions of his painter's soul, hidden outside, exposed in the studio, under fluorescent light, before an easel.

I have now left the waves of sadness and self-pity far behind to focus on the hands of my husband-artist. The hands that hold me as well as the brush that has created this work of art. It is these hands, this soul, that reach out from the painting and travel through the wake of my disturbance to pluck me from its center and to lift me up and away from my current sorrow. "There, there," they comfort me. "Do not feel sad. There, there." ▪

THE SMALLEST DENOMINATION

IN COLLEGE, I WAS A BLOCKED WRITER, ALTHOUGH I wouldn't have characterized myself that way at the time. If writing was difficult for me, I thought it was because I was a bad writer. I was confused about punctuation, had trouble finding the right word, and stumbled over how best to combine the words I was able to come up with. It was that simple.

Only it wasn't.

By the time I settled into my dorm room in Andrews Hall and sat down to write my first term paper, which happened to be in world history, I was much more than a bad writer. Although I no longer recall the topic I chose to write on, I do remember sitting night after night in front of my typewriter, yanking sheet after sheet of paper out of the platen and crumpling them up. By the time the due date arrived, I must have devoted over twenty hours to composing the paper, fifteen of those full of hand wringing and deep sighing as I struggled to coax my ideas onto the page.

After that, the pattern was in place. The minute professors assigned papers for the semester, I began working on them, typically weeks in advance. I'd start happily enough by heading to the library and the card catalogue to do my research. There

I would pore over what other people had written, not so much for their ideas, as for their words, their sentences and paragraphs, their commas and semi-colons, all in the proper place, calculated to help the reader grasp just what it was the writer was saying.

Once I'd digested whatever books I could find on my chosen topic, I'd draft an outline. This research phase might take a week or two, depending upon the subject, and by the end of that time, I usually felt pretty confident about what I wanted to say. Then, research completed, one evening after dinner, I'd gather a stack of typing paper, sit down at my desk, click open my IBM Selectric case, slide the robin's egg blue typewriter onto my blotter pad, poise my hands over the keyboard and . . . .

I should really back up a bit. The truth is that I began worrying about the papers I would have to write for each course on the very first day of class, the moment the professor passed out the syllabus. Before I even glanced at the readings, the topics to be covered during the semester, I fumbled with the pages handed to me, searching for just how many term papers the professor required and when each was due. By the end of the second week of classes, at the latest, I felt as if an avalanche had come roaring down upon me, burying me under a mass of blank pages I was required to fill with my thoughts. Thirty pages altogether for my world history class, which meant two term papers of fifteen pages each; another thirty for my course on Flaubert and Balzac, these divided into three papers of ten pages each; only twenty pages for sociology, and that wasn't due until the very end of the semester; and oh, dear! ten three-pagers for my psychology course. How would I ever be able to complete the semester's work?

Every semester I worried chronically, not only about each paper individually, but about the collective papers required of me. This meant that setting to work on one paper, I carried with me the weight of all the others I had yet to write. How to focus on Flaubert, when World War I was bearing down upon me? And close at its heels were the Bodhisattva and the myth of the eternal return.

I always knew what I wanted to say, it was the how to say it that eluded me. How to sculpt an opening paragraph when the next ten pages clamored for attention? How to proceed from the first to the second paragraph when my sentences were so sinuous that I couldn't decide just where to place my commas? And should I perhaps use a semi-colon instead of a comma in the last clause of the four-line question I posed? Or should it be two sentences? Or three?

Only years later did I begin to see that this was difficult, not because I was a poor writer, but because I was trying to scoop out individual words and sentences from a deluge that was sweeping me away as I strained to write. Struggling valiantly against an overwhelming current, I managed to complete all my papers, and did so on time. But the strain was obvious, judging from my professors' comments: *You have a fine mind, it's too bad you can't write. You can think, but you sure can't write. Good ideas, poor execution.*

If I was able to complete my work each semester, it was because I was majoring in French, a language in which I was fluent, and for some reason — which I never questioned at the time — I experienced no difficulty writing in that language. In fact, quite the opposite; many of my French professors complimented my writing. This meant that by my junior and senior years, only half my term papers had to be written in English, which reduced my torment by fifty percent.

By the time I graduated, writing even thank-you notes in English required three to four drafts, and I assumed that writing would be forever slow, laborious, painful, each word plucked from the very marrow of my bones. By the time I marched up to retrieve my diploma, "poor writer" had become part of my identity, settling in alongside "French major," "tennis player," "from Philadelphia," and "curly hair." Well, perhaps not alongside but hovering above the other tags. Four years of struggle, underlined by professors' unanimous comments, pushed "poor writer" into the foreground of my consciousness, appearing whenever I paused or slowed down, like a swarm of gnats, darkening the sky around me.

What I've told so far is the beginning of my story, or if not the beginning, the section of the plot that presents the crisis. For the resolution, we can move at a clip through graduate school in French Language and Literature, where I continued to have no difficulty writing in this other language, until we arrive at the years I taught French literature at a small liberal arts college, where I landed an office next door to Mary Swander. When I first heard her talk to her students about their writing, I remembered that in junior high and high school, not only had I written poetry, but two of my poems had been published. Recalling this in no way altered my view of myself as an inherently poor writer, nor did I wonder at my having forgotten completely about this episode in my life. But it did occur to me to try my hand at verse once again.

We can now fast forward three years. I am living in Iowa City, a student in the Poetry Workshop at the University of Iowa. I am a writer, admitted to the most prestigious M.F.A. program in the country. I stroll along elm-shaded streets, spend hours each week in the building that houses the English and philosophy departments at the foot of the campus hill, not far from the University library. My poems are discussed in workshop, where my instructors and fellow poets take what I write seriously, believing my poetry worthy of consideration, and at times of praise.

What happened?

To understand my trajectory, we now have to fast forward again, many, many years. For it took me that long to understand. In fact, it took me that long even to wonder at my transformation, to begin asking myself how, indeed, it had been possible. How had the Jane Anne Pomerantz, who could "think but not write," become

Jane Anne Staw, poet? And after that, Jane Anne Staw, writer of nonfiction prose?

Many factors, of course, contributed to the transformation. When I began writing poetry, I was no longer a student, dependent on my professors for feedback, but a professor myself. The tables had turned, and it was I who had turned them. Along with my situation, my self-image had morphed. No longer a timorous student, I was a capable teacher who stood in front of her classes and illuminated for them metaphors in the poetry of Baudelaire or the structure of a novel by Balzac. I was independent of my parents, earning a living, living a life competently on my own. All of this, I'm sure, contributed to opening the door to writing.

But in the end, I believe that it was nothing as large — or as abstract — as the situation or self-image that gave back to me the right words and the orderly sentences that had been there all along, waiting patiently, to allow me to express just what it was I thought and felt and saw. Nothing as large as timing or opportunity. What changed my life was a possibility I had never encountered before, either due to my own anxiety or the culture that surrounded me. A possibility that rubbed against the grain of ambition, that thumbed its nose at the big picture, at thinking ahead, at projecting into the future.

Poetry is the universe of small. Poems are not written stanza by stanza. They are not even composed verse by verse. They arrive on the page word by word. One word follows another, and another word follows those first two, until enough words align themselves to express a thought or an idea or to assemble an image. The pace of poetry is slow. When you write a poem, you have constantly to stop and ask: *this word or that? a comma or enjambment? new verse or continue the line? new stanza or new verse?*

The moment I set out to write my first poem in twenty-five years, the avalanche dissolved, the swarm of gnats evaporated. At long last, a space opened up for me, a clear, luminous, fragrant space, where I had all the time in the world to write. With that first poem, writing became a private act, an intimate relationship between me and the page. Nothing mattered but each word, a jewel I could examine from up close or afar, peer into or tip to reflect the light, tilt this way and that, roll about in the palm of my hand, rub against my cheek, or lick with the tip of my tongue. Each word was mine and mine alone, chosen in the fullness of time with care . . . with love.

As a poet, I did not write "poetry." I wrote this poem and then the next. Setting the words of the first line in place, I thought no more of the end, or even the next stanza or verse, than a spider casting out thread after thread anticipates the completed web. Beginning, I had no idea where I might end. Any one word might draw me in, become the heart, the pulsing center of the poem I would eventually write. For the moment, and for the duration of my writing a single poem, I would remain present with each word, allowing it its complete resonance, waiting until it cast its full light, before I moved on.

Since then I have written entire essays, even books. And if I have been able to do this, if I have continued deepening my relationship with writing and learned to spin longer and longer webs, it is only through the grace of poetry, which gives me permission when I write to think and feel in the page's smallest denomination: one word, then another word, then another. ∎

Myopic Horticulture

It's December in Northern California and my green and tidy garden of last May and June, full of fresh, young shoots and leaves and tender blossoms, is now a morass of barren stems, sodden foliage, and bloomed-out plants that have flopped over face down in the mud. I stand at my back door shaking my head. It's the same story every year. In the spring, as my perennial bed wakes up, I feel a rush of excitement and competence. I relish each new bud and blossom, first the exuberant orange geums, next the heavenly blue nepetia, followed by the egg-yolk orange of my day lily. In the weeks before, I pluck out any weeds that have pushed their way up during the rainy winter months, turn rich compost into the soil, and complete any last-minute pruning, so that each plant is perfectly prepared for its seasonal run.

But always, somewhere near the middle of July, I feel myself losing ground, and I begin to despair.

I don't know why this should be so. If I am energized and eager when the garden first starts blooming, and I spend the first minutes each morning deadheading, weeding, fertilizing with fish emulsion, then stepping back and admiring, why does the day always arrive when I want to throw up my hands in dismay?

I take a hard look at my perennial bed and everything about it looks off: the scale, the shape of the plants, the number of blooms, the colors. How is it that within twenty-four hours, my garden annually metamorphoses, at least in my eyes, from a delight to a ragtag collection of neglected plants?

It's possible that this sudden shift in my garden's appearance has less to do with me than with the geometry of growth. It might well be that a day or two earlier, my garden did indeed appear lush and vibrant, alive and prolific, and what happened is simply the result of an inevitable seasonal accumulation. Somebody more gifted in mathematics could probably devise a formula for what I experience every July, measuring each plant's capacity for height and width and number of blooms, a number beyond which the plant heaves to one side or flops over awaiting rescue.

But this tidy explanation for my garden gone amuck is probably creative rationalization. More likely, I backed off in anticipation of overwhelm, ever so slightly at first, but increasingly over the course of a week or two, as the garden burgeoned, so that I had indeed fallen behind in my tending. Perhaps without realizing it, the amount of maintenance necessary felt a bit heavy one morning, and I thought to myself: *I'll wait until tomorrow when I have more time.* And that moment, when I first hesitated and postponed, marked the beginning of the garden running wild.

It isn't that I admire manicured gardens. I find them precious. Rigid. Unnatural even. Unlike most tourists, I do not particularly appreciate the Boboli Gardens and those of Versailles. I prefer the profusion of the cottage gardens of the English countryside, stretches of plantings where yarrow rubs elbows with roses and delphiniums, and hollyhocks rise as a backdrop to lamb's ears and dianthus and sweet William. I crave the appearance of abundance and energy. Too much evidence of forethought in the garden interferes with my pleasure. What makes me happiest is a bed that seems charged with its own direction, so that the scene before me appears at the same time natural and orderly, as if the outcome was never a foreordained conclusion, but one of many possibilities, each expressing at the same time a deep level of intentionality and spontaneity.

If anything, I am a novice gardener. My Philadelphia suburban childhood did not prepare me to get dirt under my nails. Growing up, the only gardener I knew was my Aunt Anna, my favorite aunt, who lived in Utica, New York, and cultivated a postage-stamp-sized plot by the railroad tracks behind her house, filled with beefy color-saturated zinnias and lacy cosmos.

None of my parents' friends gardened, although the summer I was ten, my father cultivated four tomato plants near a south-facing wall of our house. Each evening when he returned from work, even before mixing his martini, he ambled up the drive and into the backyard to check on the progress of his plants.

Our neighbors didn't garden either. When I entered high school, we moved to a house where closely cropped lawns and trimmed hedges — all green — formed the neighborhood landscape. By the time I began college, the only plant I could name was pyracantha, a shrub that grew along the side of our house, which my mother cut and brought inside for floral arrangements.

No, a green thumb is not part of my inheritance. Nor is knowledge of the life-cycle of plants. Unlike for many of my friends, owning a home for me was not synonymous with planting a garden. It wasn't until I was divorced and on my own that tending my own patch of vegetables and flowers became important to me. Perhaps the fact that I came so late to gardening explains my gardening self-doubt and this morning's annual December despair about the sodden state of my perennial bed.

But then I remember a conversation I had several months ago with one of the long-time members of a French circle I belonged to until our beloved leader died last summer. At Sally's memorial, Anne and I began talking gardens almost immediately. "My garden's completely out of control," I announced.

"Mine's a mess too," she responded.

We continued our horticultural *Miserere*, until a smile spread across Anne's face and she announced that she'd just thought of a way to avoid our mid-season garden breast beating: "Why don't we concentrate on one plant at a time!" she said. "Each morning, we could tend our gardens with the idea of working on only a single plant, offering that plant everything it needs — nourishment, deadheading, pruning, space. This will allow each plant to come into its own," she continued. "And it will prevent overwhelm."

"One plant at a time," I repeated. "Brilliant."

But I quickly forgot our conversation, and within days I had launched into desperate and brutal pruning, followed by breast beating and misery. "Enough of rust," I declared and chopped down most of my purple hollyhock. Yellow-orange is too garish a color; it screams over all the other hues, I decided, yanking out my Mexican marigold. By the time I had cut the fuchsias down to tiny nubs, my garden resembled a battleground, piles of discarded plants and stems tossed willy-nilly.

It wasn't until this morning, months after that conversation with Anne, that I actually reflected upon what she had said. *One plant at a time*, I thought, and realized that was precisely the way I operate each spring. While my plants experience their initial growth spurt of the season, tender, young leaves unfurling, buds swelling and unfolding, I peer at my garden through a close-up lens. Too early to step back and take in the whole, spring offers up the parts to my attention. And as long as the garden has space to grow, I spend my time bending over the ground-hugging perennials in the front, or stretching toward the taller plants at the back of the border. It is once the garden has filled in that I am pricked by discomfort. With one perennial overrunning the next, the near view has to make way for the panorama. No more discreet observation of individual plants; instead, the entire garden at a glance.

But at a glance is not my mode. I'm a gazer; my vision is slow to absorb whole spectacles. When required to do so, I become rattled, suffering from sensory overload. The opera is wasted on me. As the curtain rises on the opening act, my eyes dart from the chorus to the stars to the backdrop, to one member of the chorus, then another, and back to the stage set, unable to focus or find a place to rest. Within minutes, I feel frazzled and confused. Better for me to stay home and listen, eyes closed, to *Aida* in the quiet of my living room.

I'm not at my best in groups of people either. Arriving at a party, I stand at the threshold, gazing at a swarm of guests, the buzz of conversations filling the air, panicked about how to navigate the scene and how to work my way into a group. And once within a circle, how to find an opening for speech. I once met a woman who confessed she had taken a course from The University of California Berkeley Extension on how to enjoy parties, so I know I am not alone in my experience of social overwhelm.

Even smaller groups can daunt me. I've still not found my way within a book group I've been a member of for quite some time. My impulse is to relate to the women singly, as individuals, and not to the collectivity. Yet once we are settled in a living room and the discussion begins, the voices and comments form a hedge I can't seem to find my way through. The group becomes a blur of personalities and voices I barely recognize.

I have always been most comfortable one-on-one: sitting across from a friend in a restaurant or café, hiking side by side in Tilden Park, driving to San Francisco with one other person to see a play. Work, family, politics, books, health — it doesn't matter what we talk about. This is the rhythm where I can find my beat. A call-and-response where I know just when to speak and when to hold my tongue. A psychic space filled with just the two of us, my friend and I, where we can focus exclusively on each other, and when it's her turn, I can provide her with everything she needs to thrive — attention, understanding, empathy, and love. One person at a time. ▪

Only a Word or Two

As I was preparing to teach "The Beast in the Jungle" to my writing students, I realized that the trouble with John Marcher, the protagonist of the story, is that he thinks way too big. Within the first pages, Henry James tells us that Marcher has lofty premonitions about a turn his life will someday take, though what this turn might be and when it might take place are unknown. As he confides to May Bartram, it's something he will have "to meet, to face, to see suddenly break out in my life; possibly destroying all further consciousness, possibly annihilating me; possibly, on the other hand, only altering everything, striking at the root of all my world and leaving me to the consequences, however they shape themselves."

The very vagueness of the future event looms so large in Marcher's life and takes up so much psychic space that Marcher can think of little else. Since he doesn't at all know what this event will look or feel like, he decides he must remain ever vigilant, alert, viewing everything that comes his way as a possibility. It is to this sense of himself and his destiny that Marcher devotes his life, waiting, waiting, waiting for this something to manifest.

Along the way May Bartram joins him as witness to his waiting and in hopes of sharing with Marcher what they come to name "the truth about you." Each time I read the story, when Miss Bartran agrees to watch alongside Marcher, I long to cry out a warning to her: *Please, don't waste your time. Nothing is going to happen. This man you are joining in anticipation of something taking place is empty. He thinks much, much too big.* But of course, I exist on the other side of the fourth wall from the self-sacrificing May Bartram, and so I remain silent.

For the next twenty pages, John Marcher and May Bartram spend their time watching and waiting and talking in the most elusive and vague language about what they are waiting for. Years pass in this state of heightened anticipation, and finally, May Bartram dies. But not before she "sees" John Marcher's truth, a truth she refuses to reveal to him because it is so unbearable. It is only much later in his life, after years of travel in an attempt to escape his sorrow, that Marcher understands. She, May Bartram, is the "thing" that was to happen to him. The event that was to befall him was to have someone of great value enter his life and for him to remain blind to her presence, to her exquisite closeness to him year after year.

In the final pages of the story, while Marcher bemoans his fate, I, along with any astute reader, realize how great his misunderstanding and, paradoxically, how little would have been necessary for Marcher's life to have taken a quite different turn. The smallest of movements, the slightest narrowing of perspective would have allowed the truth to shine for him. All that was necessary was that Marcher look directly in front of him, or slightly to his side, and take in the loyal presence of May Bartram, a woman willing to devote herself, even to sacrifice herself, completely to him. A mere glance in a slightly new direction. Or a few simple words. Not the "Have you seen it yet?" he repeats again and again. But, *I appreciate you. I see what you are doing for me.* If instead of looking off into the future and perpetually taking the pulse of the wider world, he had allowed himself to feel the beating of his own heart, he might have given life back to his long-suffering companion, to say nothing of himself. It's not difficult to grasp how Marcher's grandiosity robs him of his life. It is more difficult for most of us to recognize our own impulses toward grandiosity. This is because our tendency to think too large about our lives often disguises itself as shame or anger toward ourself for not being successful, ambitious, or perfect enough. We make a mistake, perform poorly in a social or professional situation, forget an appointment, say something we regret, and we not only have difficulty moving beyond our mistake, we poke and prod at our failing until it has swollen beyond all proportion.

I know this escalation process well. Let one disappointment, one rejection, one failure, one worry come my way, and I am off and running. If a class I teach doesn't go as well as I had hoped — not even an entire class, but a dicey interval when the discussion lags and my students sit silently before me while I can think of nothing inspiring to enliven them — darkness descends. Instead of thinking that I might simply need to restate one of my ideas so that my students can better engage with me or the concept I'm trying to illuminate, I quickly conclude that I have made a terrible mistake. And my mindset rapidly escalates from there, like a wave gathering force, until it swallows everything in its path. Within moments, I am chastising myself: *Your last class wasn't all that stellar either; you're a lousy teacher; you'll probably lose your job; no one will want to hire you after that; what made you think you knew how to teach; you've never been good at anything; you're a failure.*

While preparing to teach the James story, I realized, to my surprise, that I actually share a great deal with John Marcher. Although my train of thought might at first glance seem radically different from John Marcher's, its movement is identical. Instead of focusing on what is happening at the moment, I expand the context, simultaneously stretching it back to the past and pushing it ahead toward the future. Not only is class falling a bit flat in the here and now, but for years I have not been teaching effectively. And if gobbling up my past isn't bad enough, I throw the lasso off into the future, certain I will lose my job and most likely remain unemployed for the rest of my life.

I seem to be an expert at enlarging one moment, then filling it with enough emotion and importance to consume my entire life. And the paradox is that to do this so successfully and efficiently, I must have an inflated sense of who I am. Why else would every second of the classes I teach loom so important? Why else would I decide that my students expect nothing but brilliance from me? To harbor such beliefs, to assume that my students' expectations of me run so high, I must have cultivated quite a grand sense of my gifts and my stature in their eyes.

Just as John Marcher fails to embrace fully the life he could indeed be living, I allow my own brand of grandiosity to eclipse any possibilities that might lie before me. By not narrowing my view and isolating the momentary lag in class enthusiasm, by inflating the importance of every moment of class time and my second-by-second performance, I push myself into an abyss of despair and must expend all my energy scaling out of it. How can I expect to encounter inspiration, or even insight, at the bottom of the pit where all is darkness? How much better it would be to remain on *terra firma*, to channel my energy into teaching the remainder of the class. By limiting my losses, I might open the space for a new thought to drift my way or give myself pause to listen more closely and appreciate fully what my students have to say.

John Marcher and I are certainly not alone in our grandiosity. Most of us get carried away with our own emotions and experiences at times. As humans with the capacity for self-reference, it's unavoidable. Putting ourselves at the center of the universe is something we do quite naturally. Not long ago, a friend of mine said something hurtful to another of our friends. She didn't intend to upset our friend. In fact, she had been in the process of comforting the friend about something that had gone wrong in her life. But in trying to soothe our friend, she alluded to an embarrassing event in our friend's life that had found a happy resolution. Immediately, the friend took offense. "Why did you have to remind me about that awful mess when I'm already feeling bad? How could you be so thoughtless?"

For days after the incident my friend felt disconsolate. "She'll never trust me again," she lamented. "This will be the end of our friendship." When I tried to suggest that she talk to our mutual friend, she renewed her jeremiad. "Even if she forgives me, how can I forgive myself? I made her life harder at a difficult time. I'm responsible for much of her unhappiness." No matter what I said, my friend could not get beyond the incident. "How could I have been so stupid? What's wrong with me?" she repeated, again and again.

If on the surface, my friend was demeaning herself, her self-flagellation found fertile soil in a kind of grandiosity. To listen to her, she was the most important ingredient in our mutual friend's unhappiness. And her thoughtless remark was important enough to terminate a long-standing relationship. Instead of receding into the past, the moment of her indiscretion loomed larger and larger, until there was no longer room in her vision for the friend she had upset in the first place. In the end, our mutual friend called and apologized for her own outburst. "You meant well, I was just too upset at the time to see it," she said.

I have a photo my husband took of me when we were hiking in southern Utah. I'm standing on a sandstone ledge three-quarters of the way up a massive rock formation in Horseshoe Canyon. Surrounded on all sides by red rock, with a strip of blue sky at the very top of the photo, I appear comically small. Yet I remember our hike that day and how alive and robust I felt after hiking down 835 feet to the canyon floor, then several miles into the canyon, where we viewed some of the most spectacular Indian rock art in this hemisphere.

I keep the photo nearby to remind me of my tendency to inflate my importance and to illustrate my rightful place in the world. The photo of my tiny self reminds me how, like John Marcher, when it comes to my own life, I easily think too large and misperceive proportions. ∎

THE KINDNESS OF STRANGERS

"YOU'RE SUCH A KIND PERSON, YOU DON'T HAVE TO PAY for your cheesecake," the young woman behind the counter said.

"No, please, let me pay," I protested.

"Absolutely not," she beamed at me. "I couldn't accept payment from someone as kind as you."

"No, please. I want to pay," I insisted, wanting to tell her that she had me all wrong. I'm not kind. My motives are not altruistic. I was simply in a hurry. Impatient. What you perceived as kindness, thoughtfulness, even compassion was annoyance, plain and simple. So take the money. I don't deserve your gift. I should be punished, not rewarded!

But confronted by the server's sweet face, I said none of this. I simply thanked her, then left the shop with my cheesecake and my remorse.

I had gone to the bakery that morning to grab a bite to eat on my way to a meeting. It was late and I was hungry. As I took a minute to gaze into the case, deciding what to order, a man in a motorized wheelchair rolled up to the register.

The man, a neighborhood fixture, spends his days rolling up to clients of the local eateries and coffee shops and pestering them to buy his watercolor paintings. Although he can't speak, he gets his message across: *I'm going to haunt you until you say yes*. Several months ago, just a few weeks after I had already purchased two watercolors from him, he approached me yet again. When I told him I couldn't afford his usual five dollars, he became indignant, shaking his head and grimacing.

In the bakery that morning, this same man was in line ahead of me. *Darn it,* I thought as soon as I saw him. *This is going to take forever!* While the man ordered, with a series of grunts and gestures, my annoyance intensified. He was going to make me late for my meeting!

I was pleasantly surprised when within seconds the server reached over the counter to hand the man a bag with his two muffins tucked cozily inside. "Can you take this?" she queried.

He shook his head in the negative, then made her understand, with a series of head jerks and hand gestures, that he wanted the bag placed on the table just outside the door.

"Sure, I'll set it out there for you," she replied cheerfully.

This is ridiculous, I thought. *I'll never get to my meeting.* But this is not what I said out loud. By the time I spoke, the nasty thought had morphed into: "I'll take it for him." Without waiting for a response, I plucked the bag from the server's hand and headed out the door, where I deposited the bag at the closest table.

"Would you mind opening it for him?" the server asked as I re-entered the shop.

"No trouble," I practically sang, masking the annoyance building inside me. A full five minutes had passed since I'd arrived, and my meeting was due to start any second.

As I walked back into the bakery to place my order, I heard the server saying to the man, who was still parked in front of the register, "Sure, I'll be happy to bring a glass of water to your table."

"I'll do that," I chirped. "And by the way, I'd like a slice of apricot cheesecake," I added, tossing the words over my shoulder. My initial annoyance had now swelled into anger, its wellspring a fusion of my unpleasant interaction with the man several weeks earlier and my own tardiness that morning.

When I next entered the bakery, for the fourth time that morning, I was seething, the man having asked me to remove his blueberry muffin from the bag and place it on a napkin in front of him. Then, at the very moment I crossed the threshold from anger to fury, the server held out my cheesecake and refused to take my money.

Five feet outside the door, I hesitated. I should really go back in and confess. Not only was I unkind, I was a practiced hypocrite. While thinking nasty thoughts, I made every appearance of being thoughtful and cheerful.

Ever since I was quite young, I have been concerned with truthfulness. The lightning rod for my early guilt around lying seems to have been my younger brother, born when I was not quite four and a half. When he was three months old, my mother became ill and needed to hire a nurse to help with his care. As was the custom those days, she called the appropriate agency and asked them to send somebody to our home. Two hours later I was playing outside our garden-apartment complex when an old lady doddered up the steps to our apartment. Scarcely two minutes later, she hobbled back down.

Why had she exited so quickly? Was my mother suddenly better? When I ran inside to ask, my mother explained that, no, she was still ill, but that the nurse sent by the agency was too frail to care for a near newborn. "I wouldn't feel safe," she said.

"Then what did you tell her," I queried, alarmed that my mother might have hurt the old lady's feelings.

"I told her it took her so long to arrive that I called somebody else," my mother replied.

"But that's a lie," I cried, horrified.

"It's not a real lie," my mother explained. "It's a white lie. It's O.K. to tell an untruth when you don't want to hurt a person's feelings."

I wasn't at all convinced. From my vantage point, my mother had told a full-blown lie; another nurse was not, in fact, on her way to our house.

Not more than six months later, I had a second encounter with lying, this one more intimate. My mother used to administer to my brother and me a daily dose of a multiple vitamin called Homocybrin, a viscous, tangy, orange liquid she'd pour into a teaspoon each morning. One day, feeling grown up and responsible, I asked my mother if I could give my brother and me our vitamins.

Sometime later, she checked to see if I had done so. I hadn't. But before I could form the word "No," I heard my own voice pipe up, "Yes, Mommy, I did."

I had told a lie! And from that moment on, for what felt like months, I was plagued by what I had done. Over time my guilt intensified, swelling and pulsing within me, until I convinced myself that my brother was going to die because he had missed one day of his vitamin dose. Not only was he going to die, his death would be at my hands. It was all my fault; not only had I forgotten his life-sustaining vitamins, I had lied about forgetting. If I had only told the truth, my mother could have easily remedied the situation, and my baby brother would not be in danger. Even worse, he was in more danger with every day that passed.

Why had I told what became in my mind such a heinous lie? If I had been so troubled by my mother's white lie only several months earlier, what in the world could have prompted me to engage in behavior I so clearly viewed as wrong? I don't think it was out of embarrassment for having made a mistake by forgetting. More likely, it was because my mother had bestowed upon me an honorary responsibility, and I had blown it. My role as the only beloved child had terminated once my baby brother appeared on the scene, and I immediately selected a new part for myself: perfect little mother. I had taken on the role with ferocity, beseeching my mother to let me burp the baby, change his diaper, push him in his pram, and now, feed him his vitamins.

So, that morning, with no premeditation, I let the lie slip from between my sweet soft lips and immediately began struggling with the agonies of guilt. For weeks, I could barely think of anything else. Lying down for my rest in the afternoon, I tossed and turned, wrestling with my sense of shame. In the playground with my little friends, I grappled with what I had done. At the crest of the slide, in a kind of fugue state, I would forget to launch myself downward, until my companions called my name. Once, swinging, I lost myself and let go, scraping my entire back when I landed.

Finally, one night in bed, I felt my tiny body about to explode from the pressure of the lie, which had fed on my guilt until there was no more room for it to grow. My mother had gone out to a meeting, and my father was in the living room, lying on the couch and reading. Suddenly, I could stand the fire in my belly no longer, and I rushed out, sobbing, to confess. I don't recall what my father said to me. But I can still see the lamplight shining on his gentle smile, and I remember that he lay his book down on his chest and took me in his arms.

I was absolved. Washed clean. My agony was over.

After that, I became a strict practitioner of the truth, careful never to blur the blunt edges of reality. To this day, I am completely inept at any degree of spin. I am much more likely to bend the truth against myself. It feels safer to me that way. Perhaps that is why I felt so disturbed by my hypocritical behavior this morning. Or if not by my behavior itself, by the server's misperception of my selfish motives.

I told my friend Sandy about the incident as we strolled to our cars after the meeting. "Maybe the server needed to believe you were kind," Sandy suggested. "Maybe her entire day will be brighter because of you!"

"Perhaps," I replied. "But that doesn't really take me off the hook. I'm still left with my own guilt."

Later that day, taking Daphne for a walk, thinking about how angry I had become at a helpless, if annoying man in a wheelchair, I realized a small shift in perception might have avoided all the unpleasantness. Instead of fuming internally at the man that morning, thinking about the time he was costing me, I could have brought my attention to any number of other places: to the display of baked goods in the cases, the plump slices of quiche, crumbly scones, moist cranberry bread; to the flow of traffic on the sidewalk outside, young mothers, their toddlers trundling along beside them; couples with their dogs trotting on extended leashes. Or to the server herself. I might have gazed at her blond, loose curls, her amber eyes, and thought, *Why don't I help her out? She's here all alone, and I can save her the trip outside.* If I had transferred my attention away from myself and my needs, the server's kindness might have softened my mood. A shift, which involved nothing more than looking away from myself and toward the world, might have melted my impatience and triggered my compassion. Then, when the server offered me a free slice of cheesecake along with a compliment, I would have earned it. And when I replied, "Thank you! That's really kind of you," I could have meant it. ∎

What My Father Taught Me

WHEN I FIRST FOUND OUT THAT KEITH, A FORMER student and now friend, was near death from AIDS, I was afraid to visit him. So afraid that I put the possibility of a visit out of my mind. But it wouldn't stay there. Keith had called me several times over the last months, and although I spent quite a bit of time talking to him on the phone, I had not gone to see him. It's difficult now for me to remember what I was so afraid of. Perhaps it was as simple as the unknown. I was afraid because Keith was dying, and I knew nothing about death.

My maternal grandparents died when I was too young to be aware of my mother's grief. Many years later, my dear paternal grandfather, Joe, took his last breath before I was able to fly from Ann Arbor, Michigan, to Manhattan, where he lay in the hospital after his second severe heart attack. My grandmother faded slowly from life over the next five years, until it seemed that for her there was no longer a great deal of distance between living and dying. She died so slowly over the period of a year that her death was not a discrete event.

Or maybe my fear of visiting Keith was born from thinking I had no control. In those days, I believed that once death took

SMALL: THE LITTLE WE NEED FOR HAPPINESS

over, or even began to claim a soul, we humans had very little recourse. In most cases, the doctors had done all they knew how to do, intervened with all the heroic surgeries, or administered all the powerful medications in their arsenal. Often patients had been intubated, placed on respirators, and subjected to multiple surgeries, chemotherapy, and radiation; some even received bone marrow transplants. In some cases, they had been brought back from the brink of death, sometimes more than once, before they finally succumbed. And if death is stronger than anything we humans have invented or devised, what then could I do but sit idly and uselessly by the person's side, waiting for the inevitable?

Keith's garden finally made it possible for me to visit him. Keith was a landscaper and had created a magnificent garden, which I had never seen, at the house where he lay dying. I had heard about Keith's work in the garden for some time, as he had told me about the exotic plantings he was putting in, the contours he was creating, the textures and shades of green that were taking root. All varieties of grasses and succulents, towers of jewels and forms of plectranthus beckoned me if I visited Keith, I realized one day. If I got too upset, I reassured myself, I could retreat to the garden.

But it turned out I didn't need the garden. I found my comfort sitting beside Keith and holding his hand in mine, soothing him when he was wracked by a terrifying vision. "Don't worry, Keith, I'm here," I found myself saying, in my softest, most gentle and loving voice. "I won't let that mean woman you are afraid of hurt you. You don't have to be afraid, Keith. The people who love you will stay with you and protect you."

I wasn't present when Keith breathed his last breath; that happened several days after I had last spent the afternoon by his side. But I was there when he was close to death, and I wasn't afraid. I was surprised, in fact, at how calm I remained and how intimate our time together felt; I gave him my full attention, and

126

nothing mattered except Keith and soothing his agitation, which at times was great.

I don't remember how long I stayed. What I do remember was that my time with Keith felt like a meditation, watching him breathe in and out, speaking to him softly and with great tenderness, brushing the back of his hand from time to time to remind him that I was with him. Not a terrifying time, but a sweet, sweet interlude. Death was no longer a voracious black hole. It was the intimate time I spent with Keith before he left this world.

Several years later, my former next-door-neighbor died of lung cancer. This time, I was there when Lucy breathed her last breath, although I didn't witness her passing. She had been comatose for several days, and it was my turn to spend the night with her in the hospital. For an hour or so after all her visitors left that evening, I stroked Lucy's arm and sang to her from the Lucinda Williams album she had introduced me to, belting out our favorite song, "I Lost It," several times in succession, because I knew that would please her.

Although Lucy didn't respond, I sensed that she heard me and enjoyed sharing these songs and these memories with me. I reminded her that her son, Lincoln, had learned the words to every song on that album. I talked to her about that Indian summer September afternoon when we sat on her front porch, her stereo turned up loud, and we sang along with Lucinda, our feet dangling over the armrests of Lucy's Adirondack chairs.

When I finally pulled out the sleeping chair, late, late that night, I sat for a while watching Lucy's chest rise and fall with each slow breath. Then I must have fallen asleep, because the next thing I knew, the aide had thrown all the lights on and was announcing, "Miss Lucy, Miss Lucy, it's time for me to take your vitals."

I knew instantly that Lucy had died. When I looked, I saw that her chest was still.

She had been breathing the whole time I sat by her side singing and for the fifteen minutes I watched over her from the chair on the far side of the room. But she was breathing no more. *So you wanted to die privately*, I thought. *You didn't want me there watching you.*

I had no doubt Lucy had waited to die until I fell asleep. Still making decisions about her life — and death — she needed privacy to leave this world; she slipped away sometime after I sang the last verse of the last song on the album, and my own breath deepened into sleep. She listened and waited for me to drift off, until the moment was right for her. Then she released her final breath.

When my ninety-year old father was diagnosed with advanced esophageal cancer, my fear was about his suffering, not about his dying. Now acquainted with death and dying, I felt comfortable in their presence. I knew that no matter what happened, I would be with my father in the last weeks and days, the final hours and minutes. And no matter what transpired, no matter what twists and turns his illness took, I expected no surprises as far as my own responses and reactions were concerned. I was strong. I wouldn't flinch. I would attend to him, do all I could to ease his suffering.

Perhaps it was arrogance that led me to believe I knew what to expect. Certainly it was ignorance. My father has always been a man of vision and imagination, able to think and plan far in advance of most people, even his fellow scientists. While other astronomers laughed at him, he set up a station at the South Pole to observe solar activity. Now, fifty years later, along with an observatory for studying outer space, named for my father, the Pole is the prime research location for studying the skies.

In less important ways, my father saw into the future as well. He took up skiing in the 1950s, well before most Americans had discovered the sport, and became an avid skier at Europe's most famous resorts. He skied so much ahead of his time, in fact, that the sport caused him a bit of trouble. My father was once in Ottawa, collaborating with a Canadian scientist who was an avid skier. One weekend my father's colleague invited my father along to the slopes. *Why not?* my father thought. That day, my father was hooked. Wasting not a minute, he bought skis, poles, and boots, and for the remainder of the collaboration, headed for the slopes every time he had the opportunity. At the end of his time in Canada, he boarded the Montrealer, a train that once ran between Washington, D.C. and Quebec, checking his ski equipment in baggage before he boarded.

By the time the train arrived at Grand Central Station in New York City, my father felt restless, so he got out to stretch his legs and walk along the platform until the train took off for Philadelphia. As he wandered here and there, he had the strange feeling that he was being watched. But he brushed this off as a touch of cabin fever. Two hours later, at 30th St. Station in Philadelphia, he stepped out of his car and was heading for the baggage claim, when two plainclothes detectives stopped him. "Are you Martin A. Pomerantz?" they inquired.

"Yes, I am," my father responded.

"We'd like you to accompany us. We have some questions to ask you," they informed him.

"Do I have a choice?" my father joked, certain that this was all a mistake.

It turned out that somebody had been smuggling gems over the border from Canada, and the stakeout at the train station in Ottawa had become suspicious of my father carrying his ski equipment, since so few Americans at the time skied. The stakeout had notified their American counterparts, who were certain they'd find gems hidden in my father's boots.

They didn't. And after great apologies, they drove my father to our suburban Philadelphia house, bidding him a warm goodbye and good luck.

My father has many such stories of his adventures biking, scuba diving, conducting cosmic ray research in India before many Americans traveled there. So it was no surprise that he did not gently accept the limitations forced upon him by age. Before he let go of driving, he returned three times to the DMV to have them retest his vision. He became frustrated with himself each time he could not promptly recall an arcane word. And despite his failing eyesight due to macular degeneration, he continually re-equipped his computer so he could remain active via the Internet, trading stocks and bonds, studying prospectuses, rising each morning at 6:00 for the opening market.

I expected my father to react with nothing short of rage at his cancer diagnosis. I was prepared for his fury at the prospect of his increasing fragility and now inevitable downslide. It's one thing to be ninety and know you are going to die soon, and quite another to know that you have a particularly ugly disease working full time to number your days. It's one thing to feel weak because you are old and another to feel weak because you are dying. I expected my father's reaction to this colossal news to be enormous.

But when we brought him home from the hospital where his cancer had been diagnosed, instead of railing, my father looked around the living room, taking in the artifacts from his travels set on the side tables and shelves: the wooden statue of a Bharatanatyam dancer from Delhi, the polar bear from Greenland, the crystal vase from his honorary doctorate in Uppsala, the lithograph from Hungary. He smiled. "I have nothing to regret," he mused. "I've lived a full life. I've done everything I wanted and hoped to do. Now I can just sit here and enjoy every moment I have left."

My father was true to his word. And I have come to see that what he said that day, the first day of the end of his life, is the ultimate proof of his vision. From that day forward, instead of thinking far into the future, as he had always done, he continued to cast his eyes into the present, to what surrounded him in the here and now: my brother, my mother, and I, each bite of food, his nightly Netflix movie. He lived as fully as he was able, day by day, hour by hour, minute by minute, until he died. ▪

PART THREE:

WIDENING THE CIRCLE

One Yoga Pose

For someone who has lived in the Bay Area for over thirty years, I've taken astonishingly few yoga classes. Many of my friends practice yoga regularly, and have for years. Others are on-and-off-again practitioners. But most Berkeley women, no matter what their age, have devoted a substantial amount of time to yoga. Which means that whenever anyone asks me about yoga and I reply that I've taken a total of five classes in my life, I'm met with surprise. "You've got to be kidding," people say. "You've lived in Berkeley, and that's all the yoga you've done?"

But the exercise regime I began following several months ago requires that once I've finished my exercises, I spend ten minutes relaxing in a yoga pose called Shavasana before getting up and stowing my exercise equipment.

My friends tell me Shavasana is the final pose of a yoga routine. Having exercised every muscle in your body, worked your sinews and your cartilage, your joints and your diaphragm, you lie down, face directed toward the heavens, hands at your sides, palms up, your spine supported by the floor beneath you. It's a moment to let your body absorb all the physical work you have just completed.

After practicing Shavasana for several weeks, I realized that each time I lay on my back, palms up, arms at my sides, legs and feet turned outward, I experienced a state more profound than simple relaxation. I felt both weightless and solid, floating in space and anchored to the floor beneath me. And I was simultaneously more present to my body and less conscious of my physical being than ever before.

I wondered if it is the contrast of intense activity followed by relaxation that evokes this striking response. Usually after exercising, I'm in a hurry to launch my day. In fact, I've always been in a bit of a rush when I exercise. Completing the circuit at my gym was an activity I considered necessary, but onerous. An obligation I wanted to push out of the way as quickly as possible so I could put my mind to the more important business of the day: my clients, my writing, my grandchildren. Once I'd finished the last station, I'd grab my house keys from the basket on the front desk and trot home, thinking ahead to what awaited me.

But lying on my mat in Shavasana, breathing in and out, and noticing my breath, I became acutely conscious of slowing down, of replacing the previous flow of tensing and relaxing of muscles with prolonged and consistent relaxation from head to toe. And I found I enjoyed this interlude between rigorous exercise and launching my day.

The culture we live in often infuses relaxation with guilt. You shouldn't be just sitting or lying here. You should be doing something productive; at the very least, cleaning out the refrigerator or dropping a load of clothes into the washing machine. Relaxing is being lazy. Don't you have anything better to do? Now, however, relaxation was not optional. My exercise regime required that I relax.

I also realized that I had not only earned the relaxation by completing my exercises for the day, but the relaxation itself was productive. According to my program's creators, the purpose of the relaxation is to boost metabolism and help build muscle.

Such outcomes seem paradoxical. We usually associate exertion and exercise, not relaxation, with muscle building. But since I experienced profound relaxation each time I assumed the Shavasana pose, I continued to rely on my initial explanations, noting that my intense response involved opposites and paradox, concepts quite at home in Eastern philosophy.

Then one day, several minutes into Shavasana, I recalled a friend telling me the translation for Shavasana was "Dead Man's Pose." A shiver shot up my spine. *I'm imitating a corpse,* I thought! *I'm pretending to be dead! How can that be good?*

I remember as a child living in India witnessing an event celebrating a living yogi's burial below ground in a wooden box. I can't recall if the box bearing a yogi was being lowered into the ground or, at the opposite end of the cycle, we watched as a yogi who had spent several weeks underground was being drawn up again to daylight. At the time, I had little understanding of what I was witnessing. I retained mainly a sense of solemnity and suspense.

But as I lay in Shavasana day after day, inhaling deeply and exhaling fully, feeling my stomach rise and fall, rise and fall, I understood that, just like the buried yogi in India, I was dead in stance only. My breathing was fuller than usual, my inhalations deeper, my exhalations more complete. I was not at all dead. I was dead relaxed!

One day, as I lay in Shavasana, letting myself relax into breathing in and out, I came to understand the full power of the pose. That day, I felt acutely the floor supporting my entire length, my head and shoulders, my spine, my calves, and heels all resting on the surface below me. And at the same time that my back was releasing all tension into the floor, my forehead, chest, abdomen, knees, shins, and toes were all opened to the gentlest currents of air passing over me, air entering the room through small gaps in the window of my one-hundred-year-old house and traveling toward the doorway of the room where I exercise. Connected to earth and sky, I felt part of everything above and below me, at home and at one with the universe. More than anything else, I felt safe.

And because I felt safe, I could lie unprotected, my palms cupped, ready to receive whatever came my way. I felt relaxed and unafraid, open and undefended, prepared to welcome the unknown without stumbling. Prepared to absorb even death, if it lay in my path.

Resting there, my most tender parts exposed, open to the energy of the universe, I thought: *How many of us go through the day hunched over against the unknown and the unpredictable, worried about the unexpected disappointments life may send our way? How many of us prefer wearing blinders than taking in life in all its messiness?*

Thinking this, I found myself letting go even more. *Here I am*, I thought, *completely calm and relaxed, fearing nothing, thinking about nothing, breathing in and out, my whole body supporting me, the heavens looking down on me. I am neither asleep nor awake in the usual sense. I am conscious and fluid, drifting and solid. I am everything at once.*

And then I realized that my practice of seeing and thinking small had offered me this vast experience of Shavasana. Bringing my mind and vision down from all that might have been within my awareness — the room, my state of mind, what lay ahead of me that day, the exercises I had just completed — to what I was doing at that very moment was yet another reward of small. Everything else had dissolved and resolved into this one, simple yoga pose. And at the same time, my experience of myself in my life and within the vast universe had enlarged beyond anything I had ever before imagined. ▪

My Largest Self

Although I have always characterized my inspiration for spending a year walking the Hopkins Street track as a voice in my head, thinking back to that moment now, I'm no longer certain. Perhaps it wasn't a voice at all. Perhaps it was just a thought that managed to catch my attention. A thought not unlike the hundreds of other thoughts flooding my mind that morning, the only difference being that it appealed to me more than the others. My mind could well have been casting about for direction or focus that day, and suddenly found it.

More surprising to me than its arrival, is the effect the "voice" had on me. I didn't question it. Even though what it demanded required a substantial commitment on my part, I surrendered instantly. In fact, as soon as I heard what the voice had to say, walking the Hopkins Street track and writing about it each morning for a year seemed to be precisely what I should do. What I wanted to do!

Up to that moment, the experience of convergence between myself and my acts was rare. As far back as I can remember, I second-guessed and chastised myself. Even in college, where I knew I was supposed to be, as I read homework assignments or struggled to write term papers, the voice — or voices — in my head separated me from what I was doing. *That's a lousy sentence; write it over,* I would hear. Or, *This paper is a bust; why did you ever pick this topic?* From without, I was enacting the part of the excellent student: I went to classes, took notes, completed all my assignments on time, studied long and hard for exams. But from within, I was divided: even if engaged in what I should be doing, according to the voices in my head, I was engaging in whatever it was — writing, reading, relaxing, talking to my roommate — the wrong way.

So I embraced the prospect of my year of walking wholeheartedly, anxious to begin. Not that the way ahead was clear to me. I didn't know, for instance, what I was to write about. The specific assignment wasn't included in my marching orders. And I'd be inauthentic to claim that this element of the unknown didn't cause me some disquiet. But the truth is, it didn't bother me all that much. Since I was already submitting to a will or a wisdom greater than my own, I believed that simply in the doing, I would figure it out.

I heard the voice around the middle of May and decided to begin my year of walking and writing June 1. To prepare, I bought a tiny, hand-held tape recorder so I could record my thoughts and observations as I walked. I also began clearing my mornings of obligations. No more doctors or other appointments before noon. And no more morning coffee dates with my friends. Eliminating these social encounters proved more difficult than I anticipated. My friends, with some of whom I'd had long-standing morning rendezvous, were not pleased. My decision, after all, intruded upon the shape of their lives too. But it wasn't only my friends who made my new schedule difficult. Cutting myself off from an important ingredient of my social nourishment felt scary. What if my friends filled their lives without me? What if, heaven forbid, they forgot about me?

In the end, the joy I felt at the prospect of engaging in activities that felt "right and good" was stronger than the anxiety stirred by canceling my morning social life. By June 1, tape recorder in hand, I was ready to embark.

"Won't you get bored, walking the same track every morning?" my friends asked. "I could never take the same route all the time." But once I started walking each morning, I discovered that the sameness was precisely the point. The track I walked is a rather idyllic space, nestled into a small valley, with a tiny park on the west end and the Berkeley hills beyond to the east. Like any regulation track, it is one-quarter mile around, but because it was built to serve a middle school, each lane is four feet wide. It was in this relatively small space that I would be spending at least forty-five minutes each morning.

I quickly realized that the constriction functioned paradoxically for me. It was the very circumscription of the space, the sameness of my route and my routine that freed me from the ties habitually binding me to the conventions of my life. In the past, when I wandered freely throughout the Northside neighborhood of Berkeley, as I frequently did, I focused a great deal of my attention on where I was headed. At the end of the block, should I turn left or right? Should I keep climbing the hill for exercise or veer off into the flats? I wasn't oblivious to my surroundings. I noticed the architecture of houses, observed and judged color schemes, assessed new home additions for their harmony with the original structure, and I noticed plants and trees in seasonal bloom.

But I often found myself concerned with how far I was traveling and how long I was taking. I also thought a great deal about what I would be doing next or for the remainder of the day, or I worried about some small interpersonal mishap from the previous day or an encounter scheduled for that afternoon. This meant I was never fully present to my surroundings and situation as I walked. At the same time, my mind was never very far from my actual location either. The necessity of eventually finding my way back home, watching for traffic, and deciding just how far to venture kept my wandering mind from surrendering to the momentum of my walk.

This habit of continually checking in to assess just where I was or wasn't and how much territory I had covered or not kept me conscious of my performance, which inevitably led to frequent reminders of what I should accomplish during that day and what I had failed to accomplish the previous day, all of this inhibiting both my ambition and my imagination. As I walked, the shoulds in my life overran the coulds and the mights.

The track, by its very containment, freed me, both to remain present and to wander. Once I committed to walking and writing every morning, other considerations dropped from my consciousness while I walked. I stopped worrying about what I needed to accomplish for the rest of the day, week, or month. Knowing I was doing just what I was supposed to be doing liberated me from my nagging conscience.

And I no longer had to be concerned with my location. Walking within a contained and familiar space, a relatively small space, I became less conscious of my physical presence in the world. I no longer needed to look ahead or behind; where I found myself at that particular moment was just where I should be. Able to shed my usual doubts and anxieties, I could drop fully into the space created by the track and the three miles I was walking.

At first, this containment allowed me to become a keen observer of what I noticed around me: the sycamore trees along Hopkins Street coming into full foliage, from the initial leaf buds to the mature broad beefy leaves; the shoots of the fennel plants on the track's west side, climbing higher as the weeks passed; the woman with the dowager's hump who ran her laps listing to her left, yet never faltered; the half-eaten apple tossed to the side.

But within the first month, something unexpected happened. As

SMALL: THE LITTLE WE NEED FOR HAPPINESS

I walked my twelve laps, I began journeying away from my present and from my physical location and farther and farther into my past. I returned to France, where at seventeen, I spent a month living with the Pautrat family on Avenue Pierre 1er de Serbie, learning to speak French and to navigate the Parisian *arrondisements*. I wandered once again among the megaliths of Stonehenge with my own family during a stopover in England, en route to India, where we were to live for a year when I was seven. As a child from Philadelphia, I arrived at the curb of 595 West End Avenue in New York City, where my grandparents lived in Apartment 3B.

Other days, I journeyed deeply into feelings and sensations from my past. One morning, a robin carried me back to a very early childhood scene: my mother was sitting on my bed, the breeze lifting the café curtain from the window behind her into the room as she recited a nursery rhyme: "I saw a little bird come hop, hop, hop/So I said little bird/will you stop, stop, stop . . . "

It must have been a spring day, which is why that morning at the track, the robin, a bird I have always associated with spring, evoked that particular sweet memory. But this memory is particularly significant because it was the first such happy memory of my mother to become available to me. Until that day, I had access only to what was negative between the two of us. Now, for the first time, an image of sweetness and light embraced me.

It was after this experience that I jettisoned my tape recorder, realizing that in the future I wanted nothing to interpose itself between the track and me. Walking my twelve laps, again and again, along a familiar route had allowed me to travel, not only far, but deep. The track became my magic carpet, lifting me from my current life and carrying me to exotic moments and untapped emotions from my past. Walking the small space of the track that year, I was able to live a grander life than ever before. I was able to assemble a fuller self than the self available to me when I began. A self that encompassed my entire life and all sides of my personality: my love of adventure, my sadness over my relationship with my mother, my passion for the French language, my joys in parenting Jonah, my inhibitions around writing, and my pleasure in observing the natural world around me. On the small space of the track that year, I discovered a fuller self than I'd ever imagined possible. My fullest self. ∎

A Single Breath

We HAD BEEN IN THE LAWYERS' CONFERENCE ROOM ALL morning, listening to the woman who had sued Stephen for fraud rattle off one lie after the other. In any other circumstance, her statements would have been comic. She claimed both that Stephen had failed repeatedly to provide her with a contract, and at the same time, that he had absolutely guaranteed her, at the very beginning of the job, before the plans were even finalized, a price for the entire project, which had later been exceeded by $250,000. She claimed she had trusted Stephen implicitly and that he had come highly recommended, but then later alleged that one of the lenders she had contacted had referred to him as a "scumbag."

As the morning wore on, I became increasingly upset. It was so unfair that somebody who told only lies could bring a suit against a thoroughly honest man, that nobody could intervene, that the justice process had to run its course, stealing time — so far one year — and money — so far $20,000 — from an innocent defendant's life.

Sometime near noon, the plaintiff's lawyer announced that he was tired of Stephen's lawyer's line of questioning and he would bar his client from further responses.

"That's unethical!" Stephen's lawyer yelled across the table. "Your questions are in bad taste. And I won't be yelled at!" the plaintiff's lawyer shot back. "If this happens once more, my client and I are leaving."

By now I was completely unnerved. This was a travesty; the plaintiff and her lawyer were spouting nothing but lies. Several minutes later, when the plaintiff's lawyer requested a short break, I decided to leave. The morning's questioning and responses had only fueled my rage, and I wasn't certain how much longer I could contain an outburst. At the previous deposition, I had laughed out loud at one of the plaintiff's responses, a sarcastic, sniggering laugh, and her attorney had threatened to bar me from attending.

Outside, in the bracing fall air, I thought I would quickly calm down. Instead, I felt myself winding tighter and tighter, the plaintiff's lies swirling inside my head, a jeering chorus I could not muffle. *Scumbag, guaranteed, trusted, $250,000.*

I decided to walk around the block before driving home. Walking, with its forward motion and visual distractions, usually helps me relax. But *scumbag, guaranteed, trusted, $250,000* followed me like a swarm of angry gnats, and I found myself traveling faster and faster, my arms pumping, my purse slapping my side. By the time I had circled the block, I was even more worked up, with as much adrenalin coursing through me as if I had been charged by a lion.

When I reached my car, I stopped and inhaled deeply before opening the door. As my chest rose and expanded, I sensed the slightest shift within me. While all morning I had become more and more tightly coiled, now I felt a space opening inside me. I exhaled slowly through my mouth, blowing the cloud of gnats away with my breath. I inhaled again, this time counting to ten. The space expanded. Exhaling slowly, I realized that what I had been experiencing during the course of the morning was a form of claustrophobia. Though my physical space had not been constrained, I had felt more and more squeezed psychologically, trapped with Stephen in the web of lies the plaintiff was spinning.

A person diagnosed with a serious illness might feel this way when she first hears the news. Because the disease is within her body, she cannot escape, cannot even distance herself from it. Once she begins to feel the pressure of the disease's relentless presence, she begins to wonder, *Why me?* And she exclaims to herself, "This isn't fair!" Soon, there may be no space within her or her life for anything but her illness.

Several of my friends have struggled against this progressive constriction after receiving a devastating diagnosis. In response, they take up or intensify a meditation practice, they participate in yoga classes, they make plans to fill any holes they perceive in their lives — vacations they have only fantasized taking, books they have only talked about writing, lost friends they have only contemplated contacting — to push against the walls of the illness.

The lawsuit, of course, is minor compared to a medical diagnosis. It is a force from without and haunts by trailing and enveloping its victims, not by consuming them from within. Still, it can squeeze the life out of you. While at first Stephen and I tried to keep the suit from pushing into the center of our lives, after several months of meetings with his lawyer, collecting documents, reading declarations from the plaintiff, we found ourselves talking about "it" all the time: when we went to bed, in the middle of the night, when we woke up the next morning. The suit became a permanent presence in our life together, ready to force itself to center stage the minute either of us had a free minute. The accusations were so wildly unfair that we continually found ourselves wrestling with the injustice.

That day of the deposition, I stumbled upon my way out. I stood beside my car inhaling and exhaling, the chorus of gnats dissipated, and I began to relax. My heart slowed, my mind settled. After several minutes, I could feel the earth under my feet and the air circulating around my body. I was once again aware of the pulse of life around me.

One breath. An inhalation and an exhalation. The contraction and expansion of the diaphragm. The intake of air through the nose or mouth, followed by the now-altered air flowing from the body. One breath, three seconds. The chest rises and falls. The air tickles the lining of the nose. It cools the inside of the mouth. It enters twenty-one percent oxygen, and exits eighteen percent oxygen and four-and-a-half percent carbon dioxide.

Normally each breath takes place outside of our awareness. Our body knows how to multitask. We can breathe at the same time we do anything else: talk, blink and think, even scratch ourselves or pet our dog. The only time we consider our breath is when engaged in a meditative practice that brings our attention there. Or when something goes wrong, and breathing becomes an effort.

Years ago, when we lived in Iowa City, I signed up for a one-day cross-country ski clinic over Christmas break. It was unusually cold that Saturday morning, and the weather, coupled with my degree of unfitness, meant that I found myself struggling to keep up with the group. By the time I got home, I noticed that I was having difficulty inhaling. More worrisome, each time I took in a breath, I felt a deep ache in my chest. Several hours later, still struggling with every inhalation, I went to the Emergency Room of the University Hospital, where I was diagnosed with cold-induced asthma.

For some time after that, I no longer took breathing for granted. Each time I exercised or engaged in a strenuous activity, I remained alert for the ache in my chest. *Will it return if I ride my bike up this hill? What about if I take up running? Swim laps at the university pool?* Then, after a while, when I didn't suffer another bout of asthma, my vigilance diminished. And it wasn't until some time later that I once again brought my attention to my breathing.

Not because of its malfunction, but because of the relief one deep breath offered.

Free divers know about the power of a single breath. With practice, some have descended one hundred meters on only one inhalation. To do this, they use techniques borrowed from Pranayama Yoga, an ancient tradition that focuses on the breath as the life force. From time immemorial, humans have understood the power of breath. In many creation myths, breath is the source of all life. In one Japanese version, breath is the source of the divine.

Breathing is an exchange between each of us and the universe. We inhale the air around us, which is released into the atmosphere by the earth's crust and created by all living things. Air is taken in through the nose, passes into the lungs and bloodstream, then is released, transformed by processes within our bodies. An exchange between the atmosphere and me, every single breath I take supports my life within the vastness of the universe. And this process takes place automatically, most of the time out of my awareness.

The mechanical act of deep inhalation and exhalation calmed me by slowing my metabolism. My jangled nerves were soothed by realizing that breath is the foundation of my life and that this foundation has always been and will continue to be taken care of for me. I felt endangered in the lawyer's conference room, but the danger was only superficial and temporary. On the deepest and most far-reaching levels, we are each sustained by our own healthy body and its relationship to the large world around us. Whether I am aware of this or not on a conscious level, every single breath I breathe signals to my body the reality of this essential truth. ▪

HOPE

ONE OF MY CLIENTS VOLUNTEERED A KIDNEY TO A member of her synagogue. She didn't know the man who needed the kidney very well, but she saw him regularly at services; in addition, he was the cousin of a good friend of hers. A diabetic, this man had been on dialysis for several years. A few months before my client made her offer, the man's health began to decline, and he and his wife had reached out to the Jewish community in their area, requesting volunteers for a kidney transplant. My client hadn't offered her kidney at the time, but one evening several months later, when she saw the man at a synagogue event, sitting on the sidelines, looking depressed and exhausted, she found herself walking up to him and offering to get tested to see if she might be a match. She had recently had a hip replaced and was still exuberant over the possibility of replacement body parts and the prospect for her of now living pain-free.

Within minutes, my client was surrounded by members of the congregation, applauding her, complimenting her on her generosity, toasting her bravery, and celebrating, in advance, the man's recovery. At the time, my client didn't know that she was the only person to volunteer a kidney to the man. But she knew how difficult it was to find the correct match, so she decided to put herself into the pool. She soon learned, however, that none of his close friends or family members came forward after the announcement had circulated. She was now officially his only hope.

When she first offered her kidney, my client was unaware of how diligently the man had been working to keep his health up. He had become a vegetarian, and on the days he wasn't in the hospital hooked up to an IV and a dialysis machine, he exercised intensely. When my client learned more about the man, she felt she had made the right decision. Here was somebody who was doing everything in his power to keep himself alive, and he deserved a break.

The first compatibility test revealed that my client wasn't a match. But that particular hospital had an exchange program: she could donate her kidney to another patient, while a different donor would offer a kidney to her friend. This arrangement had a disadvantage, however, because while my client could donate her kidney immediately, there was no way of knowing when the right kidney might turn up for the man she knew. Also, donating a kidney to a stranger didn't appeal to my client. The process felt impersonal and her connection to the man attenuated.

The second hospital rejected my client as a candidate because of her weight. The issue of her weight didn't surprise my client; it had been a long-term problem for her. For quite some time, she had planned to initiate a weight-loss regime, although she kept postponing.

My client felt bad about the hospital's rejection and knew how upset the man and his wife would be. They had been so thrilled when she volunteered. How was she going to tell them?

The night she received the news, she tossed and turned in bed, unable to sleep. Her situation was even worse than she had realized at first. Not only was she going to be the bearer of deeply sad news for the couple, she was sure that when she told them about being rejected because of her weight, they would ask her to diet and lose the extra pounds. She knew this because not only were they themselves very exercise conscious, but in the weeks she had gotten to know the couple, they had begun advising her on diet and lifestyle. After all, now her health would have an impact on their lives.

All that night she was not able to sleep, realizing that she couldn't blame them for suggesting the weight loss. It was only logical. Yet, the more she worried and the more she imagined the conversation with the man and his wife, the more my client knew that she could not lose the weight at their behest. Losing weight was deeply personal to her, something she needed to do for herself, not for anyone else, even if it would mean saving the man's life. She felt just awful. Having offered her kidney and bestowing upon the man and his wife the hope that he would be cured, she would have to take away everything she had given.

But would she? Wasn't it true that before she had approached the man at the synagogue, he and his wife had been deprived of all hope, unable to imagine living a full life off of dialysis? After all, nobody else had volunteered a kidney, even after the appeal to the larger community. And once she had offered to be tested, hadn't they been unexpectedly buoyed, believing for several months that help was on the way? Indeed, she had led them out of the sea of despair into the ocean of optimism, for they had indeed reacted that positively to her offer. And wasn't that a gift?

Now she knew what she would tell the man and his wife: "I'm so sorry," she would say. "I won't be able to give you my kidney. But I know I have given you something. Although not as large as we had originally anticipated, I provided you with the hope you needed to continue on your journey. And my wish for you is that now you will find a way to tread water until you arrive at your next moment of hope."

I have never had occasion to think much about hope, beyond

the usual anodynes and adages that I, along with everybody else in this New Age, spout. But I was quite moved by my client's story and had occasion to ponder. Hope is no small thing, I realized. Indeed, it is so large it is incalculable. Until this moment in my life, I have taken hope for granted. Not in the sense that hope is the assumed foundation upon which I live. Far from it. I grew up in a family of pessimists, where the worst-case scenario was perpetually prepared for. No, I have always taken hope for granted, because as a concept or a perspective, it is so frequently bandied about with so little thought. *Let's hope for the best. I hope it works out alright. You can only hope. I hope you understand what I'm saying. I hope he knows what he's doing. Hope springs eternal.*

Now for the first time, I thought about hope as a force, the energy that propels us through difficult times, carrying us from a painful situation into a future where we just may be able to see our way clear of the thickets and thorns. How else did my son's friend, diagnosed with cancer and having only several months to live, slide out of bed each morning and continue to live his life? Certainly he didn't expect a complete cure. But he must have banked on at least one good month, then a few more passable weeks, and finally, several bearable days. And when his family and friends knew the end was near, I'm certain they hoped for a peaceful passing for this good man who was being taken from them so early. It was this hope that moved them from the sidewalks of New York into the halls of Sloan Kettering Hospital, and then into the young man's room, where they stood or sat beside him during his last days, clasping his hand, speaking their love for him, and whispering their goodbyes.

Hope is the silent partner in most of our lives, the unacknowledged hero of our hours. How else would I get through a day that included working with writing clients, dealing with my aged and difficult parents, a sudden disagreement with Stephen, and a challenge from a student, along with my own personal demons, which include perfectionism and a constant inner goad toward productivity? Most mornings, as Stephen and I walk our Daphne, I embrace the day, remarking over a wisteria come into bloom, a lacey cloud formation in the southern sky. As we cover our daily route, down Posen Street and up Peralta to the alley, I listen as Stephen thinks ahead to his schedule, then tell him what I know of my day so far. I might mention a client I look forward to meeting with, or an essay I'm particularly excited about teaching. I might talk to him of a student I'm concerned about. Or worry over something hurtful my mother said. Cushioning the walk and our talk is my unspoken hope: hope that my work will go well; that my relationship with my mother, problematic all these years, will one day improve; that my student will have found her way to acceptance over my comments on her latest submission.

I have my client to thank for all of this, for my fuller understanding of how I, how all of us live our lives; how, in spite of the darkness that might surround us or lie ahead, we find ourselves moving toward the next minute, the next hour, day, month, even year; how, no matter how cruel my mother's comments, I will continue to hold her in my heart, not because I believe she will change, but because each moment of hope carries me forward in my life, no matter how my mother treats me, with kindness or not. Hope bears me along, sustains me, out of my awareness, with the belief that some things, though certainly not everything, will work out. That even at my mother's side, in the shadow of her darkness, I will be able to cast my own light. ▪

My Juliette Binoche

After nearly two days of rain, the sun had finally emerged from behind the clouds when I took Daphne out for an afternoon walk. A bit behind the shift in weather, I was still feeling glum, not from the two days of rain alone, but from an accumulation of small stresses that the hard rain had exacerbated. That evening I was to teach my last workshop of a semester that had been problematic at first, and I found myself worrying about the outcome of our final meeting. Although our sessions had been improving by the week, it felt imperative to end on a positive note. What could I do to ensure a happy ending? Or was the outcome out of my control?

When I finally noticed the dramatic shift in the light, my spirits began to lift, the way they do when you receive a bit of good news or recognize a beloved voice on the other end of the telephone. As I looked up toward the sky to confirm the disappearance of storm clouds, I heard the whirr of bicycle wheels approaching from behind me, and within seconds, a young woman, who looked a great deal like Juliette Binoche, pulled up alongside me. "Eet ees sooo buuuuteefuul!" she trilled. Then, before I could respond, she pedaled past me.

Yes, it is, I thought to myself, watching her tiny figure recede; *it is indeed beautiful.* And I took in the brilliance of the sun and the sparkling clarity of the sky washed clean from two days of rain.

Walking the remaining few blocks of my afternoon route, I held the image of my Juliette Binoche close to my heart, where she cast light on all that had been prickling me during the rain. I needn't worry about the last workshop, I realized. Over the course of the semester, its members had worked hard to become better readers of their fellow writers' work. Their response papers now contained insightful comments and penetrating questions. Equally important, the class had opened up to each other, the initial diads and triads relaxing to embrace new members, and the initial seating pattern was now shifting from week to week. There was no question about it: we had become a community of writers who offered the best of ourselves when we sat down to read each other's work.

By the time I pulled away from my house to make the drive across the Bay Bridge, I anticipated the upcoming workshop with relish. At the end of the class, I would compliment my students, let them know how much I appreciated what they had achieved. They too would benefit from my Juliette Binoche, a chance and fleeting connection — could I even call it that? — that had illuminated my entire day.

I recall another momentary encounter one morning several months ago when returning from an errand. I had turned onto a small street not far from my house, and a woman waiting in her Subaru to turn left caught my eye and smiled. I smiled in return, my smile in no way perfunctory, but a response arising from the deepest cavities of my heart. No matter that doctors and scientists might tell me that this emotion had very little to do with my heart and much more with my brain, the response I felt definitely arose within my chest, as intensely as the feelings of love for Stephen that flare within me from time to time.

How often we go about our lives disconnected, brushing past the people we come into contact with. We might offer an absent-minded nod, a flicker of a smile, but these responses, which can take place just on the edge of our consciousness, do not involve us with the people we nod or smile to in any significant way. Like a dusting of snow we quickly brush off our overcoats, the contact dissipates almost as soon as it is initiated.

Not so with the driver of the Subaru and with my Juliette Binoche. I can still see them both, in moments that transcend time, the driver's shoulder-length gray hair, her gloved hands resting on the steering wheel, her full smile; and Juliette's tiny torso twisting about on her bicycle seat as she turned to share her joy with me. Each time I conjure these moments, I feel a prickle of warmth within my chest, like a guardian angel I can summon at times of distress.

For as long as I can remember, I have struggled with fears of abandonment and exclusion. After my brother was born, I dreamed that while our house burned, my parents rode off on horseback, my mother holding my brother in her arms, as I watched from a second-story window. Later, during high school, I spent many nights wandering in my dreams among groups of girls who excluded me from their circles and conversations. Once I graduated from college, my nightmares often involved returning to the campus, unacknowledged by students who had once been my friends and unable to locate my dorm room.

My friend Eva recently suggested that perhaps these dreams were about something as profound as life and death. Evolutionary psychology, she told me, has explored the importance for women of membership in the village group, particularly while the men were off hunting. In such situations, the women depended upon one another for their very lives, and any woman who was excluded faced the possibility of death. "Your dreams mean that you're just closer to your evolutionary roots," she assured me.

I liked Eva's explanation. It released me from the humiliation my recurring dreams cause me. Aren't I too old to fear exclusion and abandonment? My parents are still alive, I've raised a son, and have an intimate marriage with Stephen; why are my dreams so regressive? Now I understand that for centuries, all women have, if at an unconscious level, feared exclusion. I am not pathetic; I am simply a reflection of my gender's deepest history. Or of every human's deepest fear.

For several years, I spent my summers in a converted one-room schoolhouse in the Amish country outside Iowa City. The setting atop a hill overlooking the surrounding farmland was idyllic: fields planted in corn and soy, days as peaceful as the lowing of the cattle and sheep, the clomping of the horses' hooves on the gravel road as they pulled the carriages of the Amish to the tiny store just beyond the schoolhouse, nights quiet and star-filled.

A truly idyllic setting, where very little ever disturbed our peace. But one summer I heard stories of a shunning, and my dreams of abandonment and exclusion intensified. I no longer remember what the shunned man had done to deserve his punishment. It was enough to know that nobody from the community nor his own extended family was to acknowledge him — publicly or privately. If any members of the community saw him on the street or in town, they were instructed to turn their head to ensure that no sign of recognition be expressed.

My friends in the Amish community didn't like the concept of shunning. And they certainly found the practice painful. But they obeyed their church and their elders and did their part in rendering the shunned man invisible. I heard later that the man had a breakdown as a result of the shunning. Well, of course. Cutting off a person's connection to community is withholding food for the soul. The community had starved this man to the point of breakdown.

Women, then, are not alone. While they may have evolved

to fear exclusion from the group as a death sentence, men are equally vulnerable to emotional isolation. Nobody can survive abandonment and prolonged psychological cruelty.

Perhaps that is why I respond so intensely to small encounters, why communications as minute as exchanged smiles and flickering greetings fill me with such sweet happiness, why they illuminate the rest of my day. If I experience my membership in community as fragile, if I struggle against the tide of abandonment so fiercely, a stranger's smile, the ecstatic words of a biker passing by are lifelines, drawing me back into the group, into the society of the village, into life. *You are not alone,* these encounters tell me. *You are not alone and you are safe.* ▪

A Glance

I don't like going to parties. Particularly those populated by strangers. Several hours beforehand, a tiny worm of self-doubt begins wriggling in my belly. At first I feel the faintest of movement, and I turn my mind to other things: a good book I am reading, weeding in the garden, even a load of wash. But as the time approaches to decide what to wear, the faint slither has morphed into a churning, burning, panicky feeling, a rusty coil in my stomach scraping my innards, and I would rather be doing anything that evening or afternoon than attending a party.

I've been telling myself that this aversion to parties is recently acquired. I haven't always dreaded them. I can remember gatherings in graduate school when I mingled comfortably with professors and other students in the French Department. Even Professor Floyd Gray, a restrained and serious man in keeping with his name, didn't daunt me. Once at a party celebrating the birthday of another professor, I saw Professor Gray sitting stiffly on the sofa across the room, and I marched over and plopped down next to him. Did I launch a discussion of the Pierre Corneille play we were currently studying in his class? Or did I make a passing comment about the fondue we had just enjoyed? I have no idea, which is an indication of my ease in initiating this conversation.

I remember parties from other epochs in my life as well: cocktails with neighbors; faculty gatherings with my then-husband's departmental colleagues at Northwestern; soirées with other students and their partners at the Writer's Workshop in Iowa City, where we writers hailed from all over the country and ranged in age from twenty-three to my forty-four years old. Far from apprehensive, I eagerly anticipated these social events, and as I recall, generally enjoyed myself thoroughly.

When, I ask myself, did parties become threats to me? When did my relationship with parties morph from pleasant anticipation to dread? And perhaps even more important, why? Why do I now worry so much beforehand? Worry that I will have nothing in common with the other guests. Worry that, once I arrive, I will not know how to slip into on-going conversations or have nothing to say. Or, if I do have something to say, it will sound thin compared to the muscle of the rest of the conversation.

Over the last few years, it's not only in my waking life that I dread parties. I've taken to having nightmares about parties as well. I'm standing among a group of people, cocktail in hand, when I realize that everyone is slowly backing away from me. Or, I'm enjoying an hors d'oeuvre, when the host storms up and tells me I must leave because she hadn't meant to invite me. Or, I cannot find my way home at the conclusion of the party, and I end up driving frantically in circles, more and more lost to my life.

I know I'm not alone in suffering this party phobia. I once met a woman at a party who told me she had attended a six-week class at the university extension on going to parties. The two of us were sitting on the sofa, our cocktails and appetizers balanced on our knees, watching the rest of the guests laugh and gesture, when I turned to her and said, "This is hard, isn't it?"

"Yea, and I even took a class to learn how to do this," she laughed. "But it doesn't seem to get any easier."

"What's your biggest fear?" she asked me.

"That what I say won't be interesting to anyone. What's yours?"

"The same," she smiled.

In my younger days, I filled my conversation with French poetry and theatre, or the history of religions. Then, when I studied for my M.F.A., poetry was a topic everybody, not only students in the workshop, found fascinating. At parties, townspeople would ask me about metaphor and simile and line breaks. If the conversation became languid, I could always exclaim, "Did you see Mark Strand's poem in last week's *New Yorker*?"

But as I've aged and the kind of social circle I was once part of has dissolved, parties have become more difficult. I have been divorced and no longer socialize with my former husband's departmental colleagues. My ex is a social scientist, and for years, his department and his discipline were a central strand in my socializing. His research and that of his colleagues was often pertinent to the larger life we all lived. And departmental and university politics were a constant in our life.

After my divorce, I moved away from the neighborhood where Jonah grew up. Away from the history we shared with neighbors and their children. Away from the collective challenges of raising children of a certain age. The problems of Berkeley public schools. Of living in South Berkeley. The swelling population of homeless, or what we then referred to as "street people," in the local business district. The shift in the complexion of Berkeley's population due to the housing bubble.

My life no longer revolves around one or two stable communities, where parties are likely to offer an ample selection of friends, or at least acquaintances to talk to. When I'm invited to parties now, I'm lucky to encounter one or two familiar faces in rooms filled with people from the host's various life communities, which are not mine — their profession, their neighborhood, the organizations to which they belong, the gyms where they work out.

Walking into such an evening, I feel a bit like I did when my parents moved to a new school district when I was in first grade. That first day, as we walked from the car to the principal's office, the schoolyard loomed ahead of me like a lion's den, filled with wild running and shouting and no place to hide.

Thinking about my troubled relationship to parties, I remembered a scene from many, many years ago. Near the beginning of seventh grade, I was invited to a party by a girl new to our school. This was the first, or one of the first parties I'd been invited to, and I remember the warmth of inclusion suffusing me when I received the invitation and happily looked forward to the event. But as the evening wore on, I became more and more upset. Nobody seemed to want to talk to me: not the boys, who were interested in a certain group of girls, those I would soon learn to refer to as "the populars;" and not the other girls, who wanted first to attract the attention of the boys, then if that failed, of the populars. I recall sitting on a chair staring straight ahead, pushing myself further and further back into the cushion, wishing I could disappear altogether, wishing I hadn't come in the first place.

When my friend's father dropped me at my house after the party, the glowing yellow light on our front porch appeared as a beacon, welcoming me back into my land, where I wouldn't have to suffer the pain of being ignored, of feeling invisible any longer. By the time my mother opened the front door, I was near tears. "How was the party?" she asked, then turned to walk upstairs to her bedroom.

"Nobody wanted to talk to me," I blurted, hoping my uttering the terrible truth would expunge what by then felt like invisible hands squeezing the breath out of me. "It was awful," I started to cry.

"You know what your problem is?" my mother asked, turning toward me and looking down from the upstairs landing.

"No," I whispered.

"You want too much attention. You want to be at the very center of everything or else you're unhappy."

For years, this memory remained underground, dormant until it found fertile ground in the more scattered community within my life and the different complexion of the parties I now attend — or avoid. Invited to a party these days, I can be quite sure I will have to expend a great deal of energy finding my way into conversations that initially will feel anything but automatic and fluid, and may well dry up, leaving me stranded.

This weekend I forced myself to attend a party where I knew only a few of the guests. I know the person who was throwing the party intimately, know the sectors of her life, and figured I possessed enough information to establish contact with at least a few of those I encountered there. For starters, I approached my friend's ex and talked about his adorable and beloved dog. I walked up to her best friend from college and mentioned a story about the two of them my friend had recently told me.

Most of the afternoon passed with me in pleasant interactions with the guests. But at a certain moment, between conversations, I stopped and looked around me. And what I saw was astonishing: one woman I had spoken with earlier seemed to be wandering from room to room alone, as if prematurely uncoupled from a larger train; two couples stood in separate corners, silently munching on appetizers, not even speaking to one another; one man studied the bulletin board of photos on a kitchen wall; and another was paging through a book he had picked up off a coffee table. And when I glanced out the back door, I saw several people in the garden, staring into the perennial bed or up into the thirty-foot pittosporum trees at one end of the yard.

I immediately understood that like me, these people are shy and awkward at parties. I could approach any of them, I thought, and open a conversation. If they are unresponsive, I can remind myself not to take their lack of response personally, not to conclude I've done something wrong. Instead, I can feel compassion toward them, as I can for myself, who so often has walked among them.

All these years I have dreaded parties. Not only dreaded before the event, but dreaded during, dreaded each next minute when I feared being forced to latch on to another conversant or to burrow myself into another group. All these years of assuming I was the only one. The only one nobody wanted to dance with. To talk to. To smile at. All these years thinking I was a failure, an undesirable.

All those years, I had assumed myself alone, the only one. I had never stopped feeling defensive long enough to look about me, to take a reading on the party as a whole. I had always assumed all the other guests were actively engaged with each other, happily cementing or even initiating relationships. But now, at last I understood my error. If I had only done earlier what I finally did yesterday: take a moment to glance about me, one moment to take in the whole, one moment to see that far from being alone, I was in good company. I was not the only person at the party who felt she had no one to talk to. There are others just like me: others unsure of themselves and the art of party-going; others who would rather isolate than risk rejection; others I could have felt, and now do feel kindred with, whom I could approach, and to whom I could whisper, "Do not feel alone or abandoned. I am here. I feel the same way. I will talk to you. I will laugh with you. I will be your friend."

All this would have been mine with one simple glance. ▪

Loving Kindness

THE EVENING I REACHED MY DECISION ABOUT NO LONGER
going out to dinner with my brother, he was even higher than usual.
In addition to the eye rolling and head jerking, several times that
night he stalled for a good minute or two cutting a piece of steak,
his knife and fork poised motionless at the edge of his plate. Each
time my mother intervened. "Here, let me help you with that. You
seem awfully tired tonight. Are you not sleeping well these days?"

What ensued was a discussion of my brother's and my mother's
sleeping problems, his periodic, hers chronic.

I've spent years trying to avoid the toxic slurry of emotions
that erupt whenever anyone mentions my mother and brother.
After that last dinner, the family situation grew even more acute.
Although my aged mother lives nearby, I decided I could no longer
participate in our family dinners.

Before that, I saw both my mother and brother often and thought
of them frequently, always with a cocktail of rage, resentment, and
hurt. My brother is a drug addict, my mother his defender. She is
also my constant critic.

That evening two years ago, after a full glass of water slipped
from my brother's hand and crashed onto the table, I realized I

could not bear one more family dinner sitting across from my brother, with his eyes rolling back in his head or alternately his head dropping nearly to the table before he jerked it up. But it wasn't only my brother's behavior that upset me. I was being forced, week after week, to pretend that nothing was wrong. My mother's unwritten rule has always involved ignoring my brother's eye rolling and head jerking and continuing to chat about this and that: her latest doctor's appointment, her noisy neighbors in the retirement complex where she lives, the last meal served in the dining room, anything other than what is going on right in front of us.

Infuse this situation with the chemistry of my mother's chronic criticism of me, her periodic global condemnation — *You're just not a nice person . . . I never wanted to live this close to you . . . Your brother is sweet; you are not* — and you may wonder why I continued exposing myself to my mother in the first place. Put simplistically, while my brother chose his path of drug addiction, I chose that of good — no perfect — daughter. No matter how many slings and arrows whizzed my way, I smiled and kept coming back.

But several days after that dinner, I veered from my habitual path. I phoned my mother and told her that I had decided it would be better if I no longer saw her and my brother at the same time. "It's just too difficult for me," I dodged.

"Then I won't be seeing you any longer," she fired back.

And she's kept her word.

After that conversation, my rage and resentment became charged with a deep grief at the loss of my family and the absence of hope for reconciliation. As the months passed, the silence from their end morphed into a vacuum so strong it threatened to suck me into its vortex.

I've spent years in therapy talking about my mother and brother, collecting insights and strategies on how to deal with them. I've tried donning imaginary space suits, erecting walls, or holding invisible shields to protect me from my mother's insults. I've burrowed deeply into the possible sources of my mother's treatment of my brother and me. As a mother myself, I can imagine the torment of watching your son become a drug addict. No wonder mothers frequently persist in remaining blind to or making excuses for behaviors others can clearly see: *He feels inadequate because of his famous father. He suffers from depression. He doesn't know how to say "no" to anybody, including himself.*

By villainizing me, my mother found an additional way to modulate her pain. Transforming me into the bad daughter helps make my brother appear less bad. Focusing on my behavior allows her to overlook a great deal of his. Telling me I'm a lousy daughter enables her to miss the needle marks in his arms. Accusing me of being selfish makes her blind to my brother's weight loss.

It might be that focusing on my flaws, even imagining many of them, is safer than facing my brother's addiction. I'm more solid than my brother, have a firmer hold on my life than he does. Criticizing him for what is actually wrong might be dangerous. He could turn on her. Or worse, turn on himself.

Making me look bad helps in other ways as well. It allows my brother to feel better about himself and my mother to feel better about her mothering. A mother bear, she attacks anything that threatens her cub. And I, apparently, am a threat. A threat because I might break ranks and speak the truth. A threat because my good life makes his addiction appear all the worse.

I understand all this. And more. I realize that standing strongly with my brother strengthens my mother's team. When my father was alive, our family frequently divided into two teams of two, which ironically helped preserve the peace some of the time. If numbers are equal, the outcome is quite uncertain. So why pick a fight? My father's death created a disequilibrium. I imagine that in my mother's eyes, I became the odd person out, and there was no longer any need to moderate her behavior toward me.

I also understand that once my powerful father died, my mother felt she had lost a great deal of standing in her world. My father was a brilliant, active man, a physicist / astronomer who journeyed to the South Pole to conduct research every year into his eighties, played the stock market, scuba dived and skied avidly. My mother's world revolved around his. She had no real world of her own. With my father gone, she must feel as fragile and windblown as the last leaf on a maple tree. If she is even more attentive and generous with my brother, he might offer at least a modicum of society as a balm for her loneliness.

After months of deep struggle and grief, I forged a fragile peace with my estrangement from my family. But last January, my mother turned one hundred, and the current toward contacting her pulsed stronger and stronger. While I knew rationally that dialing her number would result in deep unhappiness for me, I felt nearly compelled to pick up the phone. Just maybe she's missed me, I'd think; perhaps these two years have softened her toward me; how can I not phone on her one hundredth birthday?

One morning during this time, I went to an acupuncture appointment. Reading my pulses, my acupuncturist looked perplexed. "A deep divide that had nearly resolved has returned," she said, pressing more firmly on the flesh inside my wrist.

Hearing this, I began to weep and told her, for the first time, about my difficulties with my family.

She listened carefully, all the while pressing and reflecting. "You know," she said, as she lay my hand down on the tiny wrist pillow on her desk, "the Chinese who cannot be close enough to their elders to take care of them build them an altar and make an offering each day. I think something like that might help you."

I knew instantly that my acupuncturist was right. Hearing her words, I felt as if the swells of a rough sea beneath me suddenly quieted into the glassine surface of a serene lake. But how to fulfill her suggestion? I had no intention of creating an altar for my mother. Altars are not part of my culture. And even if they were, my mother didn't deserve one.

For the next several days, I felt calmer than I had for some time. Though I didn't know how, I felt certain I would find a way to fulfill my acupuncturist's suggestion. Then one day, I knew. Just like that, I knew I would devote at least ten minutes each day to the Loving-Kindness Meditation, directing it toward my mother. Having thought of this, I felt buoyant.

I have never sustained a meditation practice for any length of time, though over the years, I have periodically set aside ten to twenty minutes per day to focus on my breath. During workshops and retreats, I have also led groups of writers in guided meditation, always enjoying the collective relaxation and uplift at the end. And though I had never practiced the Loving-Kindness Meditation itself, I was familiar with it from conversations with friends and clients.

I began the very next day. Now, at least once a day, I find a comfortable seat, close my eyes, and think: *Mom, this is for you. May you be happy. May you be well. May you be peaceful and at ease. May you be filled with loving kindness.*

When I first began, I felt a great stirring deep inside each time I thought the word "Mom." It seemed as if somewhere within me, I held a stringed instrument, a lyre perhaps, and whenever I thought "Mom," a beautiful chord sounded, continuing to vibrate for quite a while. It had been so long since I had used the term "Mom," so long since I had spoken to my mother. How much longing I had accumulated!

After a few weeks, I noticed that several images formed in my mind as I meditated. In the first image, I was walking toward a mountain with the sun shining near its peak, and as I began to approach the mountain, I opened my arms as if to embrace the air around me.

At other times, I saw myself in my mind's eye, nodding my head in complete agreement with the content of the meditation. I was nodding slowly, a smile on my lips, as if I was saying *Yes, yes, yes* to myself, in full accord with my actions and words. This is a relief for somebody who has so often found herself divided, one part pulling and the other pushing.

After continuing this practice for several months, when my friends gingerly brought up the subject of my mother and brother, I no longer felt the familiar explosion of rage and sadness. Instead, I felt happy and light. No longer crushed at the mention of my family, I found I could easily slip, "Nothing new in that department," into the conversation.

I've read that meditation can change brain waves. I've also read that it can create new circuits in your brain. I don't know whether this is what I'm experiencing or not, but directing the Loving-Kindness Meditation to my mother has created a positive association within me. It's that simple. Mention my mother and I feel embraced by loving kindness.

Several weeks ago I decided to include my brother in my meditation. Now, each day as I sit to begin meditating, I think, *Mom and Marty, this is for you.* And periodically throughout the ten minutes, I invoke my mother and brother again, just to keep them within my focus and my heart.

Since my brother became part of the ritual, as I go about the rest of my life, my mind drifts toward the family rift very infrequently. The new association with loving kindness is taking up the space that used to be filled with grief and rage. The toxic slurry has receded, the way some days the fog just inland from the Mendocino coast pulls further and further out to sea as the sun rises higher and higher, until all traces of white vapor disappear, leaving a cloudless sky.

I feel happier now. Before I began the Loving-Kindness Meditation, my mother and brother were always tugging at me somewhere or somehow. Anything could trigger my thinking about them and our estrangement: a phone call from an old friend; seeing a woman my age sharing a restaurant meal with her elderly mother; playing with my two-year-old granddaughter, who has never been with me and my mother at the same time; a robin wrestling with a worm in my garden, which reminds me of a rhyme my mother recited to me when I was quite young.

Ten minutes a day has released me from the unexpected tugs of my mother's and brother's absence in my life. No longer reminded of what I do not have, I am better able to fully appreciate what is there for me to enjoy. Each day now, I look forward to hearing the words repeat sweetly in my head: *May you be happy, may you be well, may you be peaceful and at ease, may you be filled with loving kindness.* Just that. And nothing more. ▪

One Sentence

AROUND FIFTEEN YEARS AGO, A FRIEND OF MINE WAS buried alive by an avalanche of rocks while she relaxed during a hike in the mountains. That she survived at all is the first miracle. That she left the hospital walking, after enduring several surgeries for the multiple fractures in her spine, along with months in a full-body cast, is the second. That she never doubted, once she regained consciousness, that she would live and walk again, is another.

After she walked out of the hospital, although never pain-free, she worked and hiked, and laughed and prayed, and gave parties and tended her friends to the fullest. Then about a year ago, she could tell that her back was weakening. The pain had increased, and she took a few falls when her legs crumpled beneath her. The doctors told her that she needed rods inserted up and down the length of her spine if she didn't want to be wheelchair bound for the rest of her life.

She didn't.

The surgery would last at least six hours. Afterwards, she would have to learn to walk all over again, literally one slow painful step at a time. The healing would take at least six months, and during that time, she was not to do anything but learn to walk. Any form of transportation was taboo. She was not even to ride in a car for the several blocks it took to reach her favorite shops.

My friend is a therapist who is passionate about her work, and she had to inform all of her clients about the impending surgery and the six-month recovery. Telling her patients about her upcoming ordeal and not being able to meet for six months made the anticipation of those meetings extremely painful for my friend. During the meetings her office became a crucible of sadness, panic, anger, tenderness, and fear.

I care very much about this friend, and couldn't bear thinking about what she had to undergo: the pain; the grueling rehab; the months without leaving her house, without working, without being out in the world. And I dreaded visiting her in the hospital after the surgery, seeing her lying in bed, tubes and contraptions overrunning her space, grimacing every time she shifted positions, all the vibrancy, the zest for life cut out of her.

It never occurred to me that my friend had a different perspective. So I was surprised when I went to visit her shortly after her surgery. I had just sat down in the chair beside her hospital bed, when she turned to me and smiled. "You know what the doctor said to me when I woke up from the ten hours of surgery?"

"No," I said.

"You're one strong broad."

It took a moment for her words to penetrate, so different were they from what I had anticipated. But when I grasped what my friend had said, my world suddenly fractured into a kaleidoscope of colors and shapes, all swirling madly in front of me. After a few moments, the swirling slowed and settled into an image of light and brilliant color. I understood instantly: This spectacular color and these shapes were a view of my friend's world. Carried on her words, her world had burst through mine.

My friend didn't see life as I saw it. Not at all.

I shouldn't have been surprised. I know many people who have struggled through hard times, perhaps a difficult childhood because of family alcoholism or abuse, a serious illness, or a terrible natural disaster. And so many of these people, although they lead a rich, productive life today, continue to define themselves by their past misfortune, viewing the world through the lens of their suffering.

I was one of those people. My brother has been bailed out time and again by our parents from the financial and legal repercussions of his drug addiction. Life at home was always shrouded by his addiction. Life after I left home was often sucked into the vortex of his downward spirals. My father and mother fought over my brother. My mother rejected me, the good daughter, in support of my brother. My father alternated between embracing me and pushing me aside in order to rescue my brother.

If you had asked me only a short time ago, I would have denied defining myself by these troubled family dynamics. I would have argued that I see myself as a mother, a writer, a teacher, a wife. It took my friend repeating her doctor's words and the dazzling image of her world they formed, for me to see, at long last, that everything I did, everything I have ever done, I colored by my parents' treatment of me. Every time I took a step forward, whenever I opened my arms to the future and what it might hold, I felt a tug backward, toward the past and its darkness. Optimism, pure, limpid hope for what was to come, was impossible for me. Look what had happened to and in my family.

At all times I carried the invisible cross of my parents' treatment of me on my back. I might have been unaware of my burden, but my psychic life surely resembled those men in Spain, who drag themselves during the *Semana Santa* through the streets of their village or town, a heavy, rough-hewn wooden cross on their back.

My friend carries no such cross. She does not identify her life with the avalanche, which she sees as one misfortune, a large one, that befell her. But all those rocks and all that force and all that weight didn't push away the rest of who she was. They may have buried it momentarily, but she never doubted that she would emerge fully from the pile of rocks.

It's difficult to break loose from trauma. We can struggle for years and through meditation, therapy, and bio-feedback, we can work through our most disturbing experiences. And we can believe that we have been successful. Then, often when we least expect it, in a flash, all the insights we have gathered about our situation, all the iterations of coaxing our heart rate down, of letting unpleasant thoughts enter then flow from our mind can seem for naught. A harsh statement, a loud noise, a poor grade takes us by surprise and our heart booms uncontrollably or constricts painfully. We may recover more quickly than we once did, settle our chest back to its gentle rise and fall, uncrimp the organs that collapsed and froze when we were triggered. But the dread and the fear the original experience unleashed continue to trail us. We can't always see or feel them, but they are there, keeping track, never letting us out of their sight, ready to pounce at the smallest opportunity.

I know this for myself. And I know this for the veterans I work with in a writing group at the Oakland Veterans Center. A veteran may be years away from combat, living a peaceful and fulfilling life, when a random encounter on the street or in a shop can rocket him or her back to the rice paddies of Viet Nam or a dusty road in Iraq. Often there's no easy accounting for it. Maybe the internal explosion they experience is the product of accumulation. Perhaps unpleasant experiences take hold of those of us with trauma, malingering in our psyches, until one day they break out of the space where they were churning and burst into our lives.

After my hospital visit to my friend, I thought about what her doctor had said to her: "You're one strong broad." I realized how different were my friend's vision and mine. Although she had been physically damaged by an avalanche of rocks, she continued to hold her arms open to everything life brought her way. Even a life-threatening operation fifteen years after the event didn't darken her perspective.

Until I began seeing and thinking small, I went through life squinting, always worried about what detritus might fall my way. I moved forward with my hands crossed on my chest, just in case. My friend has always walked with open arms, embracing what comes toward her. Her horizon has long been filled with light.

When I left the hospital, I was driving on the freeway thinking about that single sentence, when, as if a door had creaked open inside me, I could almost see the weight and clutter of my former habitual fear and dread begin to flow out of me. Years of worrying about what might go wrong, of bracing myself for my mother's insults, of worrying that I might make a mistake were swept away from inside me. Within a few minutes, I felt lighter, more buoyant. And when I looked up toward the horizon, that plane where the earth meets the sky appeared brighter. ▪

POSTSCRIPT

Recovery

Last night, my mother, brother, and I went out together for dinner. It's the fifth time we've done this in the past few months, and each time we sit across from one another enjoying Indian, Chinese, or Thai food, the exchange is warm and pleasant. My brother tells us about his mischievous Boston Terrier, Boo, and I tell stories about Frank, our rescued terrier combination, who except for Stephen and me, is afraid of everything and everybody. When we run out of dog stories, we segue into memories of family and friends: our Aunt Ann, my mother's oldest sister and our favorite aunt; our paternal grandfather, Joe; or our neighbors in Philadelphia, where we grew up. We talk about our father's exploits. We never dip a toe into the truly personal. I have no idea what my brother, who has moved to Las Vegas, does with his time. Nor do he and my mother know much about my daily life, aside from my outings with Stephen and friends, and excursions with Jonah.

We play it so safe, staying in the present, never alluding to the past, that if you were to compare our first dinner after my vacation from my family with our most recent outing, I doubt you'd discern any difference. What you'd see is one very old but still beautiful woman, one quite slender middle-aged man, and another woman, middle-aged as well, leaning in toward the old woman, the two holding persistent slight smiles, tossing the conversation back and forth, and the old woman nodding.

This is a scene I never anticipated. And for me it is nothing short of a miracle. All those years I went out with my family, with both parents and my brother first, then with my brother and mother only, all those dinners when I sat watching for signs that my brother had or hadn't used, anticipating another barb from my mother, wondering whose side my father was on that evening, full of self-pity and victimhood, sizzling with the tension of both wanting to slip away unnoticed and the intense desire to find a pocket of family love and cocoon myself within it. And now this.

That the daily Loving-Kindness Meditation moved me from rage to peace whenever I think of my mother seems like miracle enough. I no longer feel consumed by anger. No longer think of myself as a woman spurned by her own mother. Instead, I am someone who, despite the way her mother treated her, has traveled from bitter anger to love, a journey through the multiverse of sadness, sorrow, disappointment, frustration, confusion, and chaos. That one simple meditation allowed me to build beneath myself a solid foundation. I no longer live at the edge of a violent body of water, ready to suck me under at any moment.

Now, I am living a second miracle, a peaceable family kingdom, in which my mother, brother, and I can break bread together. But this miracle has proved more challenging to me. To arrive at the promised land after a lifetime of struggle can be frightening. Am I really there, I ask myself? If I am, how much longer can I stay? And if I stay, what will be required of me? What if I fail?

In my younger years, I noticed a recurring emotional pattern. Whenever something good happened to me, I would quickly take flight, held aloft by grandiose thoughts of my superiority. A flattering comment from a professor in graduate school, and within minutes I'd imagine myself at a prominent university, a tenured faculty member teaching graduate courses. A compliment from a friend, and I would feel myself soar, dipping toward and rising up from the crowd below me as they applaud my finest qualities.

Once, years ago, when a neighbor's husband was in the hospital with heart problems and his domineering mother came to visit, my neighbor asked me to take her mother-in-law to visit her son. "She likes you much more than she likes me," my neighbor confessed.

Within seconds, I was a layer of cumulus clouds floating over our hometown. Minutes later I had lofted even higher, and by the time we reached the hospital, I was floating dangerously close to the sun. The visit went well, and when it was time to leave, my neighbor's mother-in-law promised both her son and me a dinner of the specialty of her home state of Louisiana: red beans and rice.

I don't remember exactly when I started falling, but I remember well what I felt like once I crashed. Suddenly, I was a cesspool of criticism and condemnation. *Who do you think you are, feeling so special?* the voice in my head yelled. *Something terrible is going to happen, and you'll deserve it! Instead of gloating, you should feel sorry that your friend feels uncomfortable around her mother-in-law! You don't deserve to have any friends yourself,* the voice railed on. *You are so selfish!* By the time the voice stopped hailing insults down on me, the world had turned dark and menacing, leaving me battered and bruised.

It's been some time since I've struggled with such intensely ratcheting emotions. I've learned to accept a compliment for what it is: a series of kind words one person offers to another. I, or rather my psyche, no longer mistakes these kind words for gospel. I have learned not to invest myself so intensely with what others say.

Yet I found myself ratcheting once again after my first dinner with my mother and brother. I was so relieved at the new tone of amicability, I felt ready to throw my traditional armor into a ditch. The prospect of my lightened load inspired me to fantasize about my new family, the new loving family that would appreciate and support me, and at long last, perceive my good qualities, discovering just how wonderful I am. The family that would admit the error of its ways. The next time my brother was in town, I'd invite him and my mother to dinner. I'd take my mother shopping. Invite her to spend a night at our house!

Luckily, I didn't enact my fantasies. I managed to hold myself back, though it took tremendous strength and energy. So much of me wanted to shed the past, emerge whole and pure, sparkling with good will. But I've become wiser. And I've learned to scale down. Instead of taking something good and inflating it, I have learned how to keep such moments right-sized. How to maintain a more balanced perspective. How to enjoy, feel pleasure, even happiness and joy without becoming untethered.

Now, whenever I see my mother and brother and the encounter goes well, I remind myself of what I've learned and practiced these past few years. "Think small," I tell myself. "Think small. Don't get carried away. Don't blow this one dinner out of proportion. Don't aggrandize. Yes, it was a lovely evening. Sitting across from your mother who no longer eyes you sternly, who doesn't say anything critical or hurtful feels like a balm. And your brother is a great guy when he's sober; he's funny, lively, and compassionate. Of course you want to embrace him, tell him how much you love him, how you've missed him all these years. How you hope you two can become closer now that he isn't using. That you have so much to share.

"But wouldn't such a large response mean losing yourself? Leaving this lovely, sweet evening behind and propelling it forward into the vastness of the future? Instead, why not simply stay with the evening itself? Enjoy it, even thrill to it! Remember your mother's sweet smile as you told her something quite ordinary about your day. Your brother as he looked you in the eye and said, 'Gee, it's good to see you, Sis.' The three of you enjoying your curry together. The silken feel of the chai as it flowed down your throat. Forks clinking.

"All of this is good. And real. And it is yours. Who knows what might happen the next time the three of you meet? It might be lovely. It might not be lovely. But you have tonight. An experience you never dreamed would be yours. And it will remain yours always, if you simply hold on to it. Allow it to replay in your memory as often as you like, but keep it intact. Don't ask more of it than it can offer. Keep it small. Remember: one evening, a smiling mother, a sober and compassionate brother. That will always be yours." ▪

About the Author

photo: Margaretta K. Mitchell

JANE ANNE STAW has taught at the Iowa Writers' Workshop; Stanford University; for over twenty years at The University of California at Berkeley Extension, where she was named an Honored Instructor; and most recently, for twelve years, in the M.F.A. Program in Writing at the University of San Francisco. She serves on the Advisory Board of the University of California Extension Post-Baccalaureate Certificate Program in Writing. As well, she has been a Bay Area Writing Coach for the past fifteen years, working with writers on projects ranging from memoirs and historical fiction to novels, short stories, and essays. Her books include: *Parsnips in the Snow: Talks with Midwestern Gardeners* (with Mary Swander), University of Iowa Press, 1990; and *Unstuck: A Supportive and Practical Guide to Working Through Writer's Block*, St. Martin's, 2003.

CPSIA information can be obtained
at www.ICGtesting.com
Printed in the USA
BVHW04s2347130418
513401BV00005B/9/P

9 781947 067141